MW00643741

THE DEACON IN A CHANGING CHURCH

THE DEACON IN A CHANGING CHURCH

DONALD F. THOMAS

JUDSON PRESS ®
Valley Forge

THE DEACON IN A CHANGING CHURCH

Judson Press
Valley Forge, PA 19481
Fifth Printing, 1982

International Standard Book No. 0-8170-0414-9
Library of Congress Catalog Card No. 69-16388

Printed in the U.S.A.

PREFACE

This has been written to lend some assistance to those persons, pastors and laity alike, who are called upon to give leadership to the people of God in a world of change. An effort has been made to take a realistic view of the church and to face actual needs which challenge its faith and ministry. At the same time, anyone who is concerned with the "practical things" of the church must take a serious interest in the biblical and theological studies that have to do with our human predicament, God's action, and the role of his people.

This is not easy to do. Custom and preformed judgments constitute part of the freight we bring out of the past but we must make a determined effort to find our proper footing. It is all too easy to lose our way. Particularly is this true in a day when the clear-cut explanations which once satisfied so many, and which seemed so secure for generations to come, have now been brought under the shadows of doubt and hesitancy which are prevalent in our day.

Then, too, the obvious needs which the servant people of God are facing are so varied and numerous that no simple panaceas will suffice. We must search for directions and guidelines continually if the church is to be true to its mission in the changing scenes of our day.

We shall endeavor to mark out in the beginning some of the biblical principles for the ministry of the diaconate. We shall then turn our attention to ministries, both old and new, in which the deacon may share and in which he may give leadership.

The study underlying this work was begun while the writer was a member of the staff of the Division of Evangelism of the American Baptist Home Mission Society. The Director of the Division, Dr. Jitsuo Morikawa, and the author's other colleagues at that time were most helpful and encouraging in a study of the deacons and deaconesses in a representative group of Baptist churches.

Out of twenty-five years in the parish ministry the writer cherishes memories of many men and women of the diaconate who have served with dedication and often with creative insight in response to what they firmly believed was the call of God to them. They made the work we shared their own. They gave generously and graciously of their support and friendship to the minister and his family. Without these fellow members of the household of faith this work could not have been written.

Appreciation is due my secretary, Mrs. Anna Ford, for persevering in her struggle with handwritten notes. Finally, a great debt of gratitude is owed to the encouragement and insights of one who has walked with me through the years of ministry and is my wife, Helen McBride Thomas.

CONTENTS

THESE PEOPLE CALLED DEACONS

The place of the diaconate in the Christian church is secure. Virtually every communion provides for the office of deacon, though there may be widely differing descriptions of the meaning and responsibilities which belong to the position and differing names for it. We feel confident that matters are being handled in a properly Christian way when the deacons are seen going about their work. They assist at baptism and the Lord's Supper, care for the membership, supervise the deacons' fund, and generally undergird the work of the clergy. Everything seems snug and secure because we know the deacons; we have helped to elect them to office, and they are doing the things which we think deacons ought to do. And this is the case in virtually every church.

Not everyone is quite so confident, however. The deacons

themselves often find it to be a traumatic experience to begin working at the tasks which they feel are laid upon them both by their ecclesiastical heritage and by the expectations of those who have chosen them. More than this, a growing uncertainty about the adequacy of traditional patterns and a deep hunger to provide a ministry and leadership for today's church increase the apprehension of many, even among those who are not deacons. As persons who have been chosen to lead the church in its ministry, it is inevitable that members of the diaconate should want to know who they are and what they are to do in the face of the numerous and frightfully complex needs of the church that ministers to an age of change.

No thoughtful Christian can escape an awareness that the church is receiving a heavy bombardment both from foes of the church without and from a loyal opposition within. It is labeled as irrelevant in its message, unconcerned in its acts, confused in its purposes, and impotent in its ministries. It is said to be failing this generation because it wallows in nostalgia, keeps the troops in quarters when they should be on the front line, answers questions no one is asking, waxes indignant over things that matter but little, and passes by on the other side while humanity, beaten and robbed of its hope, looks wistfully for help.

It is no wonder, then, that concerned deacons and Christian workers are disturbed as they contemplate the responsibilities of their leadership. Some meet the problem by falling back upon set patterns, sighing in relief that a confrontation with the disturbing demands of the modern church can be postponed. At the same time others meet the problem by looking for guidance to the Scriptures, to their own traditions, and to the church. The latter are to be commended in that they continue in faith and hope to face up to the staggering needs and opportunities of our day; they continue to ask how their work can be responsive to the call of Christ today, and they ask how they can help the church to accept renewal as a gift from God for a new, dynamic, and redemptive advance.

The Puzzle of the Deacon

One of the instincts of the church is to turn to the Scriptures for guidance in times of perplexity and confusion. This is a commendable procedure, but one that frequently exacts a toll of hard, disciplined study, because the message of the Scriptures cannot always be read off the surface of the biblical narrative. Such is certainly the case when we try to uncover the origin, qualifications, and duties of the diaconate in order to be certain that in this matter we are in the true lineage of the New Testament church.

It is certain that, however ardently we may want to be a simple New Testament congregation, we cannot achieve our dream. We have changed. Many of the issues confronting the church are of a different order and of greater complexity than those of earlier ages. Moreover, New Testament and historical studies have clearly demonstrated that the early Christian communities followed varying patterns of worship and church organization. One pattern is to be found at Jerusalem, another at Corinth, and a little later there are hints of still another order in the Pastoral Epistles of 1 and 2 Timothy and Titus.

Perhaps this obscurity is good. If we should discover an original church order in its pristine purity, our determined efforts to follow it might cause us to be untrue to our Lord; untrue, that is, to his command to serve and bear witness to him, and to his desire that men should know him and his way for them. This is to say that our attention might be given to forms rather than to ministry.

It is also certain that we pick up a puzzle when we turn to the New Testament to discover how the diaconate became such a prominent group in the life and ministry of the church. The picture of the ancient diaconate does not snap into focus as we might hope. How this office originated, what these people did, and who they were are parts of the puzzle.

What were the origins of the diaconate? Just three references in the New Testament mention the office of deacon. These are Philippians 1:1; 1 Timothy 3:8-10, 12-13. A fourth possible reference to the diaconate as an office is Romans 16:1 where Phoebe is spoken of as a *diakonos* of the church that is at Cenchreae. A question arises in the minds of some because *diakonos* is a masculine term but Phoebe was a woman! But there is not a word in the Scriptures about how these positions came to be established in the early churches.

Some scholars have claimed to find the antecedents of the deacon in the *hazzan,* or attendant of the synagogue. One difficulty is that he is referred to in Luke 4:20 as *huperetes* or attendant! Elsewhere the word refers to guards or officers and not to *diakonos.* In addition, the exclusively liturgical [1] functions of the synagogue attendant do not prepare us to expect the administrative and pastoral duties which marked the early deacons.

It is futile to go into the secular usage of the word "deacon" to uncover the origins of the Christian office. Various ministrants in pagan temples were referred to as deacons in a list dating from 100 B.C. They are named among those presiding at the dedication of a statue to Hermes, and Serapis and Isis were served by a college of deacons presided over by a priest.

[1] Liturgy (from *leitourgia*) means literally "work of the people." It is not an exercise of the clergy, with the laity as spectators, but the service of God by the people in their language, and in keeping with their understanding and experience of God in Christ. But it always summons them onward to richer affirmations of their faith, deeper relationships, and more faithful obedience. It takes the form of specific patterns of hymns, prayers, readings, preaching, and ordinances by which the family of God is able to express its worship corporately in addition to the devotional life of the individual.

But merely tracing the historical use of the title for the office is fruitless because this instance is one of many in which the early church took a commonly used word, infused it with new content, and placed it in a new context.

While Acts 6 is frequently read at the time of church elections, it is difficult to decide whether or not Luke thinks of the seven persons described in Acts 6 as the first Christian deacons. It would be helpful if we knew that he thought so, because we would then know that the first deacons were set apart to their work by prayer and the laying on of hands. We would know something of their character and functions (see Acts 6:7-10; 21:8) but Luke never calls them deacons. It is true that the church in Irenaeus' day thought of the seven as deacons and that many an early church refused to have more than seven deacons. In A.D. 315, the council of Neo-Caesarea set seven as the proper number, but Luke, for his part, leaves us with the puzzle, with surmises, and nothing more.

A second part of the puzzle that refuses to slip into place has to do with the responsibilities of the New Testament deacon. Vigorous activists that we are, we could content ourselves by turning from scholarly research into the origins of the diaconate in order to inquire about what they did and what their successors have been doing. Then we could get on with the work with some sense of security. Incredible as it may appear, we cannot work it out that easily. We shall find some very helpful guidelines for those engaged in diaconal ministries later on, but let us first see something of what this part of the puzzle is about.

In the first place, the reference (Acts 6) which we have generally considered as most helpful is not one where *diakonos* is used in the technical sense of an office. Yet it has been helpful precisely because the church has sensed here an illustration both of the adaptability with which the early church met new situations and an example of the kind of open-hearted concern which characterized the Christians. This is what Luke seems to be underlining for us as if to say, "This is the way in which differing needs can be met while keeping central the care of people."

The story is a simple one of how some in the church were not receiving a fair share of the common provisions. Determined that none should be neglected and that loving concern should take the place of division and need, the Christians agreed to a suggestion from the apostles. They set aside seven men of good character to share in the ministry by serving tables (see Acts 6:3) and thus released the apostles to devote themselves "to prayer and to the ministry of the word" (Acts 6:4).

We can only speculate about the assignment given to the seven because the word "table" *(trapedza)*, while perhaps referring to a dining table, was also the word for a money changer's or administrator's table. Since we know from earlier references that the Christians were sharing their possessions (see Acts 2:44-45; 4:34-35), we dare to hazard the supposition that the seven were assuming, for a time at least, administrative responsibility for the material welfare of the Christian community. Any effort to uncover further details is futile: We are left with inferences.

We can be certain, however, that the diaconate was not a restrictive office because not many months had passed before one of the seven, Stephen, was serving also as an effective witness and the first martyr in the ministry of the Word (see Acts 6:5, 7:1 – 8:1). And Philip, also of the seven, soon became an evangelist (see Acts 6:5; 8:4-8; cf. Acts 21:8). How long this ministry of the tables was carried on is open to question, because the gifts Paul later collected for the poor at Jerusalem were not given to the care of deacons, but to the elders (presbyters) (Acts 11:30).

The places where "deacon" refers to the holder of a particular office (Philippians 1:1, Romans 16:1, and 1 Timothy 3:8-10, 12-13) are equally as silent concerning the responsibilities of the office. Perhaps they are named with the *episkopoi* (bishops or overseers) in the first reference because they shared in providing the offering for which Paul was thanking them in Philippians 4:10-18. The description of the deacon we find in 1 Timothy 3:8-10, 12-13 implies a ministry that took them into the homes of the Christians and into contact with the material resources of the church. They were to be responsible Christian workers. The last reference (Romans 16:1) suggests that Phoebe was active in giving practical assistance to those in need, but we have no other details.

It seems regrettable that the Scriptures are not more specific about the kinds of things that trouble deacons today, even in the care of those in need. There are no clues as to how to administer the deacons' fund, how to collect it, who is worthy of assistance, or how may it best be distributed and reported to the church. There is nothing recorded about constitutional responsibilities: how to interview new members, how to assist at baptism and communion, and scores of other questions. There is nothing on the surface of the records about how deacons can lead a congregation to minister in an urban, industrialized, mechanized society. Perhaps this is good. At least we cannot get so busy following blueprints and organizational diagrams of the early church that we miss other imperatives which we face today.

One other piece of the puzzle is to know who these deacons were, where they fitted into the structures of church life, and what marked out this office and those who shared its responsibilities.

If the seven of Acts 6 were forerunners of the diaconate, we know that they were men of good reputation, "full of the

Spirit and of wisdom." They were known to the Christians and were chosen by them for a specific ministry. The letter of 1 Timothy was written at a later date and addressed to a young minister in Ephesus but it adds color to the qualification "of good repute." On the positive side, the deacon is to be serious, hold the faith, be blameless, and be a good head of his family. The New English Bible lists the following as prohibitions upon him: "double talk, given neither to excessive drinking nor to money-grubbing," or things which militate against a good reputation and an effective ministry.

We now begin to see the kind of persons these were, but where did they fit into the structural pattern of the church? Did they have the one-board or the multiple-board system? Were they really leaders of the church? Were these men assistants to the higher clergy, as some have inferred from the order of "bishops and deacons" in Philippians 1:1; did they have an authentic ministry to perform on their own, as Acts 6 might imply; or was this an office which served as the preparatory school for full ordination, as is the practice in the Roman Catholic and Anglican communions? Questions like these are not clearly answered from the few references we have.

Marking the Path

When we begin to ask what marked out this office and those who bore its responsibilities, we uncover some clarity, some background, that helps us to pull the puzzle together. We can get at this best by going back to look at the Greek word from which we get our word "deacon." Variations of the verb *diakoneo* appear thirty-seven times. We encounter this in translation as: "to administer," "to minister," "to serve," and once by "serve office of deacon." The form *diakonia* is found thirty-five times and appears to the English reader as "administration," "ministration," "ministry," "office," and "service." Finally, another form, *diakonos,* translated as "deacon," "minister," and "servant," appears thirty times in the New Testament.

Broadly used as it is, this word can give the modern deacon some light on the depth and breadth of his ministry. For example, *diakonos,* or servant, is used in reference to slaves (see John 2:5, 9), a civil ruler (see Romans 13:4), and the followers of Christ in relation to their Lord as his agents or instruments (see John 12:26; Ephesians 6:21; Colossians 1:7; 4:7; 1 Corinthians 3:5; 2 Corinthians 3:6, to indicate but a few). The *diakonos* is in relation to the gospel (see Ephesians 3:7), to the fellow disciple, or to the church as a whole (see Mark 9:35; Colossians 1:25). The word describes the work of the disciples (e.g., see Matthew 20:26; 23:11), and even of our Lord himself (see Romans 15:8).

In some references *diakonia* points us to a function or office in the church such as the work of apostles, evangelists, and prophets (see Acts 1:17; 20:24; 21:19; Romans 11:13; 1 Corinthians 12:28; 2 Corinthians 4:1; 5:18). The function implied in Acts 6 involves both ministry at the tables for the good of the church and the ministry of prayer and the Word. In Matthew 25:42-44 the word covers various services for the needy. In Romans 15:25 Paul is seen serving the poor in Jerusalem by receiving a collection for them. This service to men comes into view repeatedly. Taken together, the uses of the word point to a Christian effort to meet the whole range of human need: physical, emotional, and spiritual.

It is interesting to notice that this word "deacon," which from the first has implied some form of leadership, does not carry the connotation of power or prominence. This simple, ordinary word for service is used to speak of Christ's service to men and of the service owed by one who is a Christian to God, to Christ, and to his fellows. In this way the New Testament clarifies the pastoral character which should be the mark of the church, corporately as a total people of God, and individually, both in places of leadership and in the private responsibilities one bears in life. This concept of service makes all Christian leaders servants of servants, supporting them, leading, counseling, and instructing them in their ministries. It applies to the deacon today as well as to that of the New Testament era. Service is the characteristic that encompasses all the ministries of the church.

How did this unglamorous word for service, servant, and serving become so central in describing the attitude and activity of the Christian community? Briefly put, the Christians took their Lord's life and words seriously.

For example, in one story our Lord was confronted by his disciples, who were indignant because the mother of James and John was trying to gain the promise of special privileges for her sons in the day when Jesus would come into his kingdom. He reminded them that the normal way in which men ruled over others, with pride, power, and special privileges, was not for them. Rather, the greatest among the apostles would be one who served "even as the Son of man came not to be served but to serve . . ." (Matthew 20:28; cf. Mark 10:45). Also, Luke 22:27 reads: ". . . I am among you as one who serves." His life had many facets, but his sharing of joys and sorrows, his lifting the burdens of sinful men, the hungry, the afflicted, the estranged, and those broken in the conflicts of life was one service, a unified ministry, a *diakonia.* The world, its redemption and reconciliation, its help and its healing, was encompassed by his loving concern.

Apparently the early Christians felt that they did not dare to deny his pattern of service or refuse his ministries when they had been chosen to serve in his name. He had left them an example; they should follow in his steps.

The apostle Paul caught the meaning of this figure when, in a letter to the Corinthian church, he analyzed his own ministry by saying that he did not extol himself but "Jesus Christ as Lord, with ourselves as your servants for Jesus' sake" (2 Corinthians 4:5). He came back to this basic concept of service, of diaconal relationships, in other places. With Apollos, he was a minister through whom the Christians believed (see 1 Corinthians 3:5); Paul glorified his ministry as an apostle (see 2 Corinthians 11:23) and as a servant of the gospel and of the church (Ephesians 3:7; Colossians 1:23-24). The ministry of Timothy is further described in this manner (1 Thessalonians 3:2). Compare, too, his comments about Tychicus, Epaphras, and the example of service and ministry given by the laity of the household of Stephanas (Ephesians 6:21; Colossians 4:7; 1:7; 1 Corinthians 16:15). This, then, is the background for the servant motif that runs through the whole of the New Testament.

A Motif for Today

The servant motif is often lost in a scramble for office, success, or some tangible, material recognition of an individual's worth. But if the servant pattern is really so central to our understanding of what Christians are about, it is entirely fitting that this all-too-human scramble for position should have its antidote in the persons of leaders of the congregation who are chosen as "deacons" or "servers." Persons who have demonstrated in their lives a concern for the deeply complex needs of the faithful and the world are among those who should be chosen to be deacons. They are needed in the church to lead a servant people to speak for their Lord and to serve in his place, not as overlords but as servants.

On occasion the diaconate may act on behalf of the church, and at other times it may lead the membership in its diaconal task on behalf of the fellowship and for the world. Because no group assumes specific Christian responsibility spontaneously, the deacon must give careful thought to the leadership role given him in the church. His ministry is essential for both the maintenance of the group and the fulfillment of the purposes for which it has been brought into being. Without this diaconal concern on the part of the leaders in the church no minister, surrounded by the overwhelming tide of functions which press upon him in the modern church, can keep alive the servant motif.

The diaconate has a higher calling than to fight a rear-guard action for outmoded patterns. It is in the position where it should push out the boundaries of mission and service which mark the central task of the church. Innately desirous of non-involvement, the church needs a leadership to help the people of God to minister freely and self-forgetfully to the whole spectrum of human need, in whatever ways possible, in the church and out of it, as a service to Christ.

For Further Consideration

1. To what troublesome questions do you wish the New Testament would give direct, unequivocal answers to the modern deacon?
2. How would you translate the deacon's qualifications into our language?
3. How restricted do you feel by the normative Scriptures, church practices, and the expectations of the congregation as you endeavor to minister today?

THE SCENE OF THE DEACON'S MINISTRY

We dare not consider the deacons alone, abstracted from the church and those others who are also leaders. It is within the church, in relationship with the church and somehow expressive of the life of the people that the diaconate functions. And, like all Christians, they have been assigned the privilege of ministering in the world, but the church is the immediate context within which the deacons serve.

Just to use the term "church"[1] creates different images for

[1] Church is a word descended from the Scottish *kirk,* Dutch *kerk,* German *kirche,* and the earlier Greek *kuriakon* or "the Lord's house." The New Testament word translated "church" is *ekklesia,* which refers to an assembly of people, in this case the people of God; in the local church (e.g., 1 Corinthians 1:2), in the churches (e.g., 1 Thessalonians 2:14), and in the total church (e.g., Colossians 1:18).

different people. Some think of it as a group of strange folk who gather in unusual buildings to do "religious things"; for others it is simply an institution that divides on almost every significant issue but dares not be ignored politically, economically, or socially. Then there are those who, more correctly, picture people, Christian people, as the church.

Building the Church

Christ claimed the right to build his church (see Matthew 16:18). We who are of the church have confessed Jesus Christ as Savior and Lord and believe that we have entered upon the new creation as sons of God. At the same time, we are not so brash as to suppose that our faith has earned our salvation; it is a gift of God in his grace (see Ephesians 2:1-10). Neither do we equate salvation with the repetition of certain precise phrases. Salvation is a dynamic relationship with God through Jesus Christ.

"Jesus is Lord" (1 Corinthians 12:3) may very well have been the earliest confession used at the time of baptism. Spoken as a statement of a person's conviction, it was lived out in obedience. Confessing this loyalty marked a break with one's past and a declaration of allegiance to Jesus Christ, however demanding might be the claims of one's own era, culture, or personal ambition. It is no easier for us to make that affirmation now than it was then. Even so, the Savior's will and redemptive purposes should be normative for his people, although they frequently differ radically from the standards and drives of our day.

When we submit life to Jesus Christ and his rule, we enter his kingdom, a kingdom that is not marked off by national or racial boundaries but which exists wherever Jesus Christ is Lord. We pray for this kingdom because we still do not see all creation acknowledging the authority of Jesus Christ; nor indeed do we completely yield authority to him ourselves (see

Matthew 6:10; Philippians 2:10-11; Hebrews 2:8). We have entered the kingdom, but it is yet to be revealed in its fullness.

If we follow the lead of the early Christians, we will neither arrogantly claim the authority of the kingdom for ourselves nor assume that we adequately represent the fullness of God's purposes. But we will think of ourselves as the fruit of his redemptive purpose and as persons who are in the world in the place of Jesus Christ to do his work (e.g., 2 Corinthians 5:20; John 17:18, 20-21; 1 John 4:17).

In accepting forgiveness we find a new relationship to the One who has forgiven; learning that God does not erect barriers against us, we become reconciled with him. Experiencing forgiveness, we dare to proclaim forgiveness; being reconciled, we become agents of reconciliation (Colossians 1:21-23; 2 Corinthians 5:18).

The Work of the Church

It may be right here that we find another clue for the work of the modern deacon. A number of scholars have given convincing evidence that Jesus thought of his mission as the creation of a new Israel, a people of God, members of the household of faith. He taught them a pattern of prayer, set their hearts toward worship and service, and left them with the enormous task of bearing witness, baptizing, teaching, and serving all men everywhere (see Matthew 28:18-20; Acts 1:8).

As early as the Creed of Constantinople of 381 A.D. we discover a description of the church that lives to our own day: It was described as "One," "holy," "catholic," and "apostolic." These terms may not describe any single, particular church we know, but they do give some benchmarks by which to evaluate ourselves. To describe the church as one is to remind ourselves of the "One body and one Spirit . . . , one hope . . . , one Lord, one baptism, one God" which are central to our faith. We cannot claim that any of the varieties of church life based on differing forms, nationalities, races, or other human divisions are of final importance. The church is one and it is to be holy to represent a holy God (see 1 Peter 1:15; 2:9); it is to be catholic, that is, universal, reaching to every kindred, tribe, and people.

If this vision is to be carried out, the church must be apostolic. In the world, bound up with the world in all of the world's complexity, and under the full gaze of the world, the church is called to live the apostolic life of a people sent (the meaning of "apostolic") by the living Lord. It is by doing the works of him who sends us, rather than by tracing church positions back to the apostles, that we succeed in becoming apostolic. We are called, then, to be a fellowship of people gathered about the Lord, a company of apostles whom he has sent into the world. When our faith ceases to find expression in serving and bearing witness, just then we cease to be an apostolic people.

The church is the work of Christ and is made up of those who have trusted in him. Its reason for being is that it might represent him in service and witness to our day. In these two areas, namely, the maintenance and strengthening of the Christian family and the apostolic function of that family, we find two of the chief concerns of the diaconate.

The Church as an Institution

About now we should be prepared to receive some biting questions from outside the church and severe criticism from within because of the way we have tied the diaconate to the church, highly institutionalized as it is. And, actually, we cannot quite avoid drawing the deacons just this close to the structures of the institution we call the church.

The person outside of the church, who is aware of only the institutional structures of the church, is skeptical of our claims to be a redeemed people of God knowing forgiveness and reconciliation. He has a right to his questions because, in our humanness, we cannot hide the fact that our claims are ahead of our achievements. Furthermore, since he has not experienced the presence of God in the church, he can only view the church as simply another of the institutions of our society, possessing all of the assets and liabilities of any other group but; in addition, laying lofty claim to be under the lordship of Christ.

Such claims have a hollow ring both for the person estranged from the church and for many of those in the church. It is precisely this institutional character that most hinders the work of God today. Some insist that the new patterns of church life and witness which our day demands can come into being only if the institution disappears. They even have some careful studies to support their contention that rigidity of institutional forms often stifles a church which finds itself in a world of change.

To counter these proponents of the "all new, all pure church" we have those who insist that the way forward is simply to move back to a more spiritual age. They would put to one side the insistence on a relevantly up-to-date ministry and urge us to recover some pattern out of the past: whether it be of organization, of piety, of methods, or all of them together.

Both answers to the needs of the modern church require a second look because they seem too simple. Persons who believe we should turn to the immediate past for our answers forget that much of what we once did may really not meet urban, industrial man in his situation, a situation unlike any he has ever faced. The other group cannot be asked to forgo their criticism of the church as it is today in favor of positive thinking. But they can be reminded that persons who choose to live and work together cannot easily avoid some structuring of their efforts toward common objectives.

It has become a truism that institutionalization solidifies any movement, crystallizes its objectives, hardens the lines of its structures, and moves toward absolutizing its purposes and methods. Scarcely any church avoids this tension between its life as the fellowship of the people of God and its life as an institution. We should feel very close to those of every age who have struggled with this pull between structures and human relationships, inner piety and outward service.

We get a feeling for this when we remember how Isaiah reminded the people that God was concerned about the discrepancy between their religious practices and their daily conduct in society, or the way in which Jeremiah rebuked his fellows because God expected more from them than merely a confidence in the Temple and their vociferous claim to be the people of God. Our Lord's own experience offers numerous examples of this same tension, and it is with us even now. While we cannot deny our relationship to God, we still live in a very difficult world to which we sometimes succumb.

A Question We Face

Our basic problem is to accept the fact that an institutional expression of the church will exist in some form or forms for a long time to come. Actually, if commonly held concerns of the Christian community are to find expression, some kind of structure is necessary and this is our burden. We simply must reckon seriously with how our forms of institutions are to be shaped and what major purposes they shall fulfill. Without structures the energies and concerns of the people will be dissipated. The group will neither be strengthened by redemptive, creative interaction between its members, nor will it be prepared to minister effectively in the world.

It is difficult not to be impressed by the uncertainties and ambiguity surrounding the life and work of the deacons. Indeed, this feeling is strengthened by the lack of clarity in the Scriptures concerning church organization generally, which we have already reviewed. Two tendencies may result: On the one hand, the Christians may be tempted to careless fragmentation and anarchy in matters of church polity, and, on the other hand, they may become purely pragmatic, directed by activistic impulses, transient interests, or hunger for "success."

Chaos in organizational patterns should be avoided because we need structures that assist us in communicating and cooperating with our sister churches. Working to solve mutual problems is made more difficult when the structures of participating groups vary too greatly.

At the same time, when we are structuring ourselves for merely pragmatic reasons, we are in danger of losing our souls. "It works," or "this is the road to success," or "these are the easy steps to get the job done" is the battle cry of the pragmatist. We may be forgetting meanwhile that we are called to serve and bear witness in the name of Christ. In ministry we are at the intersection of God's activity on behalf of human needs, and the human material is intractable and unrepentantly self-centered. The pragmatic, activistic approach to organizational forms is not to be decried unless such an approach causes us to misunderstand what the church is about, manipulate persons, and confuse the quest for large numbers with a ministry to the kinds of need for which Christ gave himself in life and in death. What our Lord has called us to be and do should help us to determine how we shall structure our common life.

The time has come to build upon more solid foundations. The shadowy nature of the biblical record about church organization should not drive us to frustration but to a sense of responsible freedom. We are free to reassess, to take a new look at the purpose and power of Christ in the gospel, to take a new look at what is needed now. Then we of the church may find the earlier patterns speaking to us in new ways — we may even discover that new days are calling us to quite unfamiliar ways of fulfilling our ministry.

Along with those who look on the church as a notable failure, there are others who believe that we can entertain a genuine hope for renewal and recovery of direction. They believe that there are signs of hope in our day. One of these is inherent in the gospel message of forgiveness, recovery, and wholeness. Our cynicism should not blind us to the fact that God's grace should be as applicable in the life of the church as it is in the lives of men and in movements in the world. No one will deny the need for the church to call on the name of the Lord; neither can any deny that our Lord may then actually move among his people.

Another sign of hope is found in the untapped reservoir of Christian commitment which remains in the most moribund and institutionalized examples of the church. The current emphasis on the ministry of the laity as the whole people of God is one source of hope that the church member may recover his role as God's servant in new ways and in the places where he spends his life.

Yet another ray of hope is seen in the many movements, in the church and out of it, where Christian people are trying to give fruitful expression to their faith. The fact that some of these are off to one side of the usual ecclesiastical organization has not protected them from tyranny of structures all their own. At least, however, they are trying to find ways by which the gospel may be held before the world wherever men are found and whatever their position. Their efforts run the gamut from clinic-centered retreats to discussion groups where Christians may be in the minority; from house groups to the mammoth mass meeting of the evangelist or the lay-centered Kirchentag in Germany; from the humble communion in a worker's home to the sophisticated work of the German Evangelical Academies; from denominational youth movements to world ecumenical conferences.

We dare not lose sight of the fact that there are churches where pastors and people are aware of the brokenness of humanity in a broken world, where they remain sensitive to the grace and power of God among them. This, too, is a sign of hope, although we are tempted to fear that the examples are all too few. Where signs of hope exist, we dare not despair. Resistance to change, to involvement, is a human error and not a part of the divine purpose. A truly Christian, prophetically creative ministry by clergy and laity alike may yet open the church of Christ to a vastly richer ministry in our revolutionary generation.

The deacon as a servant of the servants of Christ must be determined to understand the gospel as best he can, and also to look squarely at the realities of the world's needs. Then he will be in a position to pray that our Lord Christ will use him to bring them together by God's grace. The deacon with a realistic bent of mind reminds himself that he has entered on a continuing and rigorous responsibility. The New Testament church did not cover the earth in a week; neither was the Reformation completed in Luther's lifetime. By the same token, the needed renewal of the work of Christ in his church may not be completed in our lifetime, but it must begin now.

For Further Consideration

1. How do you view the relationship between the church as the people of God and as an institution?
2. What reasons can you see for discouragement with the ministry of the church? What can be done about them?
3. What reasons for hope can you give as you view the church and its work?

THE OFFICE OF DEACON

Some early Christians, sparsely scattered over a wide area, often threatened and sometimes suffering, received a letter reminding them that they were to administer their gifts ". . . as good stewards of God's varied grace . . ." (1 Peter 4:8-11). How varied were the ministries and gifts God gave to the church may be seen by referring to Romans 12:3-13; 1 Corinthians 12:4-11, 27-31; Ephesians 4:11-12. They were given in such profuse variety as this because the needs confronting the Christians were so numerous and varied.

God gave the strengths and abilities which his people possessed. No servant of Christ, therefore, could take pride in his gifts: He had nothing that he had not received (see 1 Corinthians 4:7). Neither could the Christian assume that he was expected to be the sole master of the gift or that he should gain private benefit from his ministry. God gave his gifts for the sake of "the common good" (1 Corinthians 12:7) and "for the equipment of the saints, for the work of ministry, for building up the body of Christ" (Ephesians 4:12).

The Call

For the sake of clarity we may say that the general call of God belongs to all Christians and the specific call sets aside certain persons for particular responsibilities. The one is inherent in our relationship to Jesus Christ and stems from the rights of the Lord to the life he has redeemed. The other has to do with the ordering of the Christian community for the sake of its coherence and functioning as a corporate body.

The general call of God is to all Christians. It is a much more profound thing than our simply agreeing to attend certain services and to give a percentage of our incomes to the church. It is a call to each of us to make the work of God our own.

We can reach into both Testaments for guidelines. The book of beginnings, Genesis, tells the story of man made in the likeness and image of God. He was placed in a creation that was good. By man sin entered the world and, so the story goes, the creation was distorted and the lives of men were marred, their possibilities blunted. The rest of the biblical story deals with God's effort to recover, to restore, to heal, to save. And now the Christian is called to make the work of God his work. Where men are deprived of their rights as men, whether it be by the blindness and ignorance of centuries or by the inhumanity of man to man, the Christians have a concern, both as human beings and as persons committed to Christian work. God has not withdrawn his creative purposes for men, and we could well adopt them as our purposes.

Turning to the New Testament we discover some very pertinent admonitions. "Let each of you look not only to his own interests, but also to the interests of others" (Philippians 2:4); and as if this simple statement were not sufficient, the apostle Paul illustrates his meaning by pointing to the example Christ has given us by the very fact of his coming to earth for men in their need (Philippians 2:5-11). Again in Galatians he urges the Christian ". . . to bear his own load" (Galatians 6:5) but to have sufficient physical, spiritual, and emotional strength left over to "Bear one another's burdens, and so fulfil the law of Christ" (Galatians 6:2). No limits are drawn, no areas of life are out of bounds to this kind of ministry reflecting the One who came to serve. In the words of the 1644 Confession of Particular Baptists: ". . . he [Christ] hath given authoritie, and laid dutie upon all, to watch over one another." [1]

In the area of what we often call a spiritual ministry it is interesting to watch the early Christians as they came under persecution: "Now those who were scattered went about preaching the word" (Acts 8:4). They believed that the intention of what we call "The Great Commission" in Matthew 28:18-20 was not exhausted in the lives of the apostles. The ministry of the Good News of salvation, of recovery and wholeness in Christ was theirs to proclaim by lip and by life. It was not the private preserve of some special class or group. Christ's call to them included his right to their service. In other words, the New Testament pictures the total congregation as involved in mission. The whole church is apostolic. The work of ministry belongs to each Christian.

There is also a specific call to ministry. This, too, is a gift of the Lord, and it is given for the common good in the work of Christ. This call may come to any of us by the voice of the church through its vote, by our confronting particular needs, by the possession of unusual gifts, or by a deep concern for the

[1] W. L. Lumpkin, *Baptist Confessions of Faith* (Valley Forge: The Judson Press, 1959), p. 168, Art. XLIV.

work of God. This call has particular functions in view, whether they be for the strengthening of the fellowship or for leading the people of God in the functional fulfillment of their ministry.

John Smyth, usually thought of as a founder of the Baptist movement, had followers who wrote in *Propositions and Conclusions concerning True Christian Religion, 1612-1614:*

> That Christ hath set in His outward church two sorts of ministers: viz., some who are called pastors, teachers or elders, who administer in the word and sacraments, and others who are called Deacons, men and women: whose ministry is, to serve tables and wash the saints' feet.[2]

In 1611 another early Baptist, Thomas Helwys, wrote of ". . . Deacons Men, and Women who by their office releave the necessities off the poore and impotent brethrē concerning their bodies." [3]

The 1644 Confession of the Particular Baptists describes the elders and deacons as responsible for ". . . feeding, governing, serving, and building of his Church. . . ." [4] In this, however, they were but an extension of, a representation of, all the Christians:

> And as Christ for the keeping of this Church in holy and orderly Communion [fellowship], placeth some speciall men over the Church, who by their office are to governe, oversee, visit, watch; so likewise for the better keeping thereof in all places, by the members, he hath given authoritie and laid dutie upon all, to watch over one another.[5]

Because the early Christians placed the importance of an office in its functions and saw offices develop out of functions, there was a flexibility in their ministries which we sometimes

[2] *Ibid.,* p. 138, Art. 76.
[3] *Ibid.,* pp. 121, 122, Art. 20.
[4] *Ibid.,* p. 166, Art. xxxvi.
[5] *Ibid.,* p. 168, Art. xliv.

overlook. Paul filled his apostolic office by special appointment from the risen Christ, but he was also a prophet, administrator, and, for short periods, a settled pastor. Peter, for another, was the spokesman for the Jerusalem church on the day of Pentecost; at another time he was a missionary.

Faced with the urgency of the task awaiting them, the Christians served in ways that ministered daringly and creatively to actual needs. They placed little emphasis upon office *per se*. Their call from God was not to formal offices but to deeply committed concern, a concern *for* the fellowship which focused upon the strengthening of the Christians, their care and edification for the common task. But there was also a concern *of* the Christian community for the world that endeavored to hold the gospel of Christ in confrontation with the world.

In order to work in the area of these concerns in specific ways, with special care, and even with special preparation, the church has raised up officers. They share in the general call to all Christians, and on behalf of the church they also carry special responsibilities.

When we are called to serve Christ, we are not left alone. Christian service is made possible by the Holy Spirit and the presence of Christ (see John 14:15-17; Matthew 28:18-20; Acts 1:8). As we have seen in Romans 12:3-13, 1 Corinthians 12:4-11, 27-31, and Ephesians 4:11-12, the gifts and ministries which the Spirit gave to the church were quite specific, down-to-earth gifts worked out both in starkly dramatic ways and in humble, obedient, and sometimes obscure service.

The Authority of Office

The absence from the New Testament of the usual term for one who governs *(archē)* leads us to believe that authority in the church rests on deeper foundations than any particular theory of government. If the Christian possesses any prerogatives, they are derived from God and from the Christian's offering of humble obedience to Christ. They are expressed in service and submission: submission of the church to ministers, of ministers to the church, and of both to the Lord of the church (see Romans 16:1-16; Acts 17:11; Ephesians 1:22).

Any church officer has several sources for his authority even though they may not be strictly defined. There is, first of all, the authority which accompanies certain specific duties assigned to the position he fills by local church constitutions and bylaws which are usually written in general terms to cover the minimal and necessary functions within the church.

Beyond such required, essential responsibilities of the office is an area where a Christian worker moves in creative concern within the accepted convictions and actions of the congregation. It is quite the usual thing for churches to mobilize their resources to meet emergency needs in the community or on the mission field without having the details of such action spelled out in the constitution. The action conforms to the unwritten spiritual mood or attitude of the congregation. This invests an office with a unique kind of authority, but a person dare not usurp or overextend such powers. The title of his office alone will not sustain him in the face of resistance or widespread apathy. Rather, the leader in such a situation is pressing out the boundaries of action to conform to the deeply held and best convictions of the people.

Then there is an authority the church officer may exercise in proportion to his moral and spiritual stature and his integrity of purpose. Even the apostle Paul acknowledged that he was spiritual father to the Corinthian church only in the gospel. He did not use the weight of his apostolic office in instances where he did not have clear guidance from his Lord; because, however strong the inner certainty he possessed, he could not serve as a leader unless there was a positive response in the congregation (see 1 Corinthians 4:15; 7:10,25,40).

Even today the authority one may exercise in the church is

derived from the accuracy with which he reflects the will and the character of Christ, but never apart from the recognition of this fact by the people. For the diaconate this means that they are called upon to fulfill the servant ministry of Christ in the church and through the church in the world.

These foundation stones of authority are sometimes found in charismatic or specially gifted and strong personalities. But by far the majority of people feel that they must serve without the benefit of a "magnetic presence." They accept their assigned responsibilities, endeavor to remain sensitive to the deepest spiritual vision of the people, and trust the Spirit of God to certify their authority for their ministry.

Unfortunately, the position of the leader is exposed to all and his use of the office will seldom go unquestioned, sometimes because he had to choose just one of several possible, perhaps unpopular, alternatives, and sometimes because there are unfortunate persons who will always have dark suspicions concerning any officeholder. Some people will question the motives of even the most committed and able leaders. To hold an office does not exempt one from misunderstanding and difficult pressures, but it can test and refine the qualities of Christ's servants.

Qualifications for Office

A few key passages will help us to understand what these qualities should be. Those who were to assume responsibilities in the congregation were to be ". . . seven men of good repute, full of the Spirit and of wisdom . . ." (Acts 6:3). Paul instructed Timothy that:

> Deacons . . . must be serious, not double-tongued, not addicted to much wine, not greedy for gain; they must hold the mystery of the faith with a clear conscience. And let them also be tested first; then if they prove themselves blameless let them serve as deacons (1 Timothy 3:8-10).

It is immediately obvious that the deacon must be one who relates well both to the congregation and to the world in his efforts to represent his faith and that of the people. In seriousness, truthfulness, sobriety, knowledge of his faith, and the central drives of his life he will give evidence of the presence of the Holy Spirit and devotion to Jesus Christ. His public life will be a true reflection of his personal life.

Quite basic is the counsel that by their service in Christ the diaconate will gain a good standing for themselves, and their own confidence in the faith will be increased. Yet the deacon must be aware that he may be wrong and that he may fail. He is human and has his own frailties and foibles. But he must remain sensitive to the nature of his ministry, which should be firm but tender, creative and forward looking but aware of the rich Christian heritage, faithful to the church but always possessed by a concern for those outside the fellowship.

Selection for Office

It seems rather clear that the members of the early church would feel at home in a local congregation as its members share in the responsibility of choosing the leader. According to Acts 6:3 the apostles told the early church to ". . . pick out from among you. . . ." Paul saw to it that elders were soon appointed in those churches he was instrumental in establishing, but this may well have been a responsibility shared with the whole community. At least, Clement of Rome at a later date referred to those who had been appointed by the apostles or other eminent men "with the consent of the whole Church." [6]

[6] Clement of Rome, "The First Epistle of Clement to the Corinthians," Chap. 44 in *The Ante-Nicene Fathers,* Alexander Roberts and James Donaldson, eds., revised by A. Cleveland Coxe, Vol. I *The Apostolic Fathers* (Grand Rapids, Mich.: Wm. B. Eerdmans Publishing Company, 1953), p. 17.

This privilege of sharing in the choice of church leaders, including the diaconate, is jealously guarded in many communions. Who the officers are and what are the procedures for choosing them may vary greatly from denomination to denomination, and from church to church.

There are some widely used patterns among Baptists. Most commonly the procedure for the election of church officers, including the diaconate and their functions, is outlined in the constitution and bylaws of the local church. This may be an adaptation of the suggestion given in Maring and Hudson, *A Baptist Manual of Polity and Practice,* or it may be a document prescribed by a state or national office, or it may have been the product of the church itself. In any event, a nominating committee is selected a month, two months, or even a year in advance of the annual meeting to prepare a list of candidates for all the offices of the church. After giving serious consideration to the duties to be carried out, the character of life and ministry of the person needed, and after interviewing those best qualified to serve, the nominating committee will present the slate of officers to the congregation at the time of the annual meeting. There is usually an opportunity for additional names to be placed in nomination. Then the people vote.

We cannot place too much stress on the importance of selecting for the office of deacon persons suited by gifts, con cern, and character. They are expected to be leaders and yet servants of the people of God. Every church needs those who will give leadership to the diaconal work of the church. Where the church has several boards, viz., trustees, missions, deacons, etc., the center of this leadership should rest with the board of deacons. In a church with just one board, whether it is known as the board of deacons, board of managers, or just "the board," the person or subcommittee of the board who leads in the diaconal work of the church should be chosen with the specific functions of the office in mind, and the nature of the ministry should be made plain to the candidate before his name is presented for a vote.

Terms of Office

The Scriptures do not tell us a thing about the length of the terms of office for church workers, but local churches, caught in the tension between a search for qualified leaders and a desire to insure stability, have arrived at some areas of general agreement.

One change in the last few decades is the move away from the older pattern in which deacons were chosen to serve for life. This practice causes difficulties when a deacon who has been ordained in one church is caught up in the mobility of our day and tries to exercise his office of deacon in a strange place, among a different people with many other ways of doing things.

Most congregations limit office holders to terms of from one to three years with the preponderance choosing the three-year term. After the limit has been reached, a member must retire from office for a period of one year, or for a full term.

In setting the policy to follow, a congregation should give careful consideration to its leadership needs. On the one hand there are obvious difficulties in limiting the number of terms officers may hold when there are few persons of leadership caliber available. However, the dedicated but untapped resources which are in every church are too often forgotten. On the other hand, there is the risk of the development of a possessive, arrogant attitude toward their rights in the office on the part of those who hold positions without time limitations.

Training for Office

A sampling of the practices of churches has revealed that

many churches are lax in preparing deacons for their ministry. Some justify this gap in education by pointing to the high quality of the men who have been selected in years past, or they declare that the duties of the diaconate are both obvious and simple. As a result, many deacons are hampered by a lack of thoughtful preparation for an office which is filled with exciting opportunities but which has been permitted to lapse into one of honor rather than of responsibility rooted in the mission of Christ.

The training of the deacon begins even before the election, when he is first approached about his serving. He has a right to expect the nominating committee to be quite clear about the depth of concern and creative leadership which should be brought to the diaconate and to convey their understanding to him. This is every bit as important as impressing upon the nominee the need for faithful attendance at the meetings and the care of routine matters of business. Any approach that is less than realistically honest is not a worthy invitation to serve in the gospel, nor is it likely to appeal to able men of responsible vision and commitment.

Upon their election, the members of the diaconate may expect the pastor to counsel them about their new role. Many ministers have helped the new deacons to discover a sense of their heritage by reviewing the history of the local church. Pertinent sections of the constitution and bylaws should be discussed carefully so that role expectations and lines of responsibility are understood clearly. The mission God has given the particular congregation in the community and through its involvement with the wider Christian fellowship should be brought to the center of the new deacon's thinking.

Some churches provide a more formal and deeper preparation by setting aside several meetings of the diaconate to study the biblical view of the church and its mission with the aid of recent books dealing with the Christian witness in our modern age. Some associations provide an annual series of studies when deacons can learn from the experiences of others, review the practices common to their office, and share their best thoughts about the future of their work. It should be noted that a valuable by-product of the association training sessions has been a strengthening of the ties between the churches.

But the training of the deacon does not end here. The work of the church has become more challenging as the needs of the world have become complex and extensive; the necessity for continuing discipline and study on the part of the deacon has become more obvious. Continuing growth can be aided by setting apart several special meetings a year for biblical-theological studies, or by allotting one-half to three-quarters of an hour in each session to study the Scriptures in the light of the demands the church should meet.

To keep imaginations active and sensitivities alert, the diaconate should plan to review the creative movements and ministries being carried out in other places. By assigning newspapers, church bulletins, and denominational and interdenominational journals to various members of the diaconate for review items of interest can be brought before the board. It would be a strange thing if any one board should know all there was to know about the possible diaconal ministries; yet at the present time very few make any studied effort to find aid in the efforts put forward by others.

Relationships Between Offices

The clergy and members of church boards and committees are alike in that they work within the context of the church, the people of God who are the workmanship of Christ, and in the world to do his work (see Matthew 16:18; Ephesians 2:10). As we have seen, the gifts of God, whether to persons as in Romans 12:6-8 and 1 Corinthians 12:8-11, or in the form of gifted persons to the church as in 1 Corinthians 12:27-28, are for the common good and are made to the body of Christians. Therefore, the diaconate must give attention to the working relationships which should be maintained with other church groups and the pastor.

A study of the constitution and bylaws and consultations with other individuals and groups will clarify where the lines of responsibility fall. Avoiding friction with others by careful planning will release energies for building up a deeper fellowship within the congregation. For example, the frequently vibrating tensions between the delegated financial officers and those responsible for diaconal ministry might be avoided if the former were consulted frequently while the deacons are planning their program. After all, both groups are working for the common good and within the ministry Christ has given his people.

By working *with* other groups in the church, by keeping them properly informed, the diaconate will be in a position to pass on something of their vision and suggestions without erecting barriers of unnecessary jealousies and hostilities. To illustrate: If the deacons have found an area of need among the youth of the community, it should be a natural thing to indicate that fact to the leaders in Christian education or to the committee on Christian social concern through formal meetings of the advisory board, or as members share their personal concerns. One board of deacons became convinced that the ministry of the laity in the church could be fulfilled only if more profound biblical and theological studies could be instituted. The board of Christian education rose to the challenge and created a series of popular and fruitful studies in biblical subjects and theological themes after the patterns of the "Great Books" series. The same open relationship can strengthen other groups in the church; and they in their turn may broaden the vision of the diaconate.

In this way a board can avoid imperialistically usurping the functions of other groups and the buildup of resentments which results. A sense of fellowship in service must be created so that tasks can be shared, differences can be honestly acknowledged when they exist, and deliberate efforts be made to surmount them. The ministry is the thing, not the aggrandizement of any person or group.

By the very nature of its assigned ministries, the diaconate is close to the pastor. Earlier books referred to the deacon as "an aid to the pastor," "a member of the pastor's cabinet," "a counselor to the pastor," or "the pastor's coadjutor." These were earnest attempts to emphasize the working bonds which link the diaconate and the pastor; and they are good, providing the deacons are more than errand boys for the minister. Theirs should be, rather, an authentic ministry, deepened in spirit by sharing closely with the pastor and interpreting to him the concerns and hunger of the laity to relate their faith to the world they know.

Instances could be cited where deacons worked only as an administrative body or a court of review. There have been groups who felt called merely to direct the work of the pastor: allotting his time, setting priorities for his work, and determining what convictions he should have and how he should express them. Other boards have served only to review plans and programs in order to be certain all the norms were being met. Neither kind of group is particularly creative or helpful in bearing the Christian witness in our very untraditional age.

Ministers are all too human for the tasks they are given. The deacon will be most helpful if he tries to think his way into his pastor's life. It is a busy life with dozens of responsibilities to be carried out every day including decisions that will affect the church, the people, his own witness, his life, and the life of his family. His is a demanding life that has exacted many years of schooling and experience beyond college and still calls for self-discipline, subordinating his life to the needs of others. Like the ancient prophets, he must wrestle with himself when he is required to speak the Lord's word of rebuke or prophetic insight to the people he loves and serves. While serving the church, he must remain sensitive to the community; living as a citizen, he must also represent the church. Anxious to be one with the people, he must accept the role of leader; called to be a leader, he must never cease to be one of the people. He will falter; sometimes he will fall; and when he does, not only his ministry is affected, but the work of the total church, the cause of Christ, is touched by it. The diaconate has a ministry to perform through a heightened sensitivity in its relationship with its pastor.

Certainly it is to be hoped that the day will never come when either the deacons or the pastor questions the motives and commitment of the other. Such a stance leaves little foundation for the erection of new structures of communication and cooperation. We need to remember that:

> There are varieties of gifts, but the same Spirit; and there are varieties of service, but the same Lord; and there are varieties of working, but it is the same God who inspires them all in every one (1 Corinthians 12:4-6).

The deacons and the pastor should permit themselves to be drawn into a unique unity, sharing, if they will, the perplexities, the heartaches, the concerns, the joys, dreams, and triumphs of Christian ministry as together they ask what the Lord requires of them.

Some pastors remember with appreciation deacons who challenged their plans with insightful questions. They were prodded to greater clarity of purpose and refinement of plans with the help of committed co-workers. By the same token, some boards can remember when an unpleasant truth was spoken by the pastor out of a concern for new developments in the neighborhood, or failure in an area of ministry, or an ingrown concern for the status quo. Such experiences are not easy to face, but they may be necessary if there is to be a mutual facing of the service that Christ has left to us. It is a simple matter to fall back on familiar patterns, on habitual statements — rather than face the struggle, the costly service that may be involved in making the gospel a living reality to modern man.

The deacons should give some thought to the relationships they and the church may have with community agencies. This can work out in many ways. Some churches have decided they will share with other agencies in areas of community need rather than indulge in costly duplication of services already being offered by such agencies as the YMCA and Boys' Clubs. One eastern church canvassed the service agencies of its area and listed the posts that volunteers might fill. As a result, several scores of Christians were deployed into the community as a service to persons, for the love of Christ.

One congregation discovered that the desperately needy people around them suffered not because of a lack of helping programs from the city, county, state, and national agencies, but because the activities of these agencies were not coordinated. The boards of the church worked to bring about a community council to coordinate and strengthen the efforts of all concerned people.

In another place the pastor and board saw the need for an increased counseling service for the poor of the neighborhood, a need which was swamping many of the pastors. Through their initiative, a qualified Christian counselor was called, and offices were set up in one of the churches as a service in Christ's name. Still another board faced this problem by enlisting professional people in the church who served as a volunteer staff in such fields as medicine, law, and finance to help meet situations which other agencies failed to meet or where deeper aid was needed.

A pastor of a Baptist church in Germany was queried by an American tourist about the doctrine of separation of church and state when he learned about the several hospitals the Baptists operated on behalf of the city. The immediate answer was, "There can be no separation of church and state in the face of human need." We could paraphrase his statement to read, "We can allow no separation of church and state, of clergy and laity, of deacons and others in the face of human need, where men need Christ."

For Further Consideration

1. What are the specific statements concerning the diaconate given in your church documents? Are there also some unwritten rules and customs that give direction to the diaconate of your church?
2. How do you feel the one engaged in the diaconal ministry can be best prepared for his work?
3. What qualities would mark the most helpful relationships between the boards and workers of your church? How can they be achieved?

THE DEACON IN THE SANCTUARY

Early in the history of the church the duties of the diaconate became centered on set liturgical functions, a condition which still exists in many communions. This fact is evident even in free churches where the deacon's most important ministry is confined to assisting in the Lord's Supper and baptism. In a few places the diaconate is being urged to enlarge the boundaries of its ministry, but, generally speaking, the performance of the serving ministries and responsibility for the worship of the congregation has passed into the hands of the clergy. The deacons have been left with a few routine functions.

An unpublished study done for the American Baptist Home Mission Society by its Division of Evangelism will make this clear. The procedure was simply to ask for a listing of the constitutionally assigned duties of the deacons from a sampling of churches of every size, from every type of community, and from at least one church in each association.

Many who returned the questionnaires confessed that the deacons were not fulfilling their assigned duties—in effect another way of saying that the usual minimal statements of constitutions and bylaws actually open more doors for ministry than many boards of deacons are entering. The slight degree of agreement which exists concerning the status of the diaconate may be illustrated by the following list[1] of the most commonly assigned responsibilities and the percentage of churches reporting each one:

	Responsibility	Percentage
1.	Assist at communion service	100%
2.	Assist at baptism	99%
3.	Provide for pulpit ministry	89%
4.	Call on sick and shut-ins	86%
5.	Administer the deacons' fund	85%
6.	Oversee the evangelistic program	78%
7.	Call on nonmembers of the church	78%
8.	Interview candidates for membership	77%
9.	Participate in pulpit committee	71%
10.	Lead prayer services	70%
11.	Lead church services	65%
12.	Take lead in church discipline	56%
13.	Prepare communion elements	42%
14.	Take communion to shut-ins	36%
15.	Share in watch-care committee	34%
16.	Instruct new members	31%
17.	Give leadership in social action	21%
18.	Serve as the pulpit committee	21%
19.	Serve as the board of missions	12%
20.	Serve as the board of Christian education	9%

There was a wide scattering of other responsibilities. Obvi-

[1] D. F. Thomas, "The Deacons and the Deaconesses," prepared for The Division of Evangelism, American Baptist Home Mission Society, September, 1960.

ously the figures are a bit hazy because some churches assign certain of these duties to the women who are deacons, to a board of deaconesses, or to other groups who may or may not have been counted as part of the diaconate. Some boards, however, do pick up an amazingly wide range of tasks by the wise use of responsible subcommittees. Other churches expressed discouragement with the actual achievements of the diaconate. One report consisted of a masterpiece of brevity, saying, "The deacons serve communion and act as the transportation committee."

A by-product of such a survey is to urge caution about endowing diaconal practices one sees in his own church with unusual sanctity, because there is simply no traditionally uniform Baptist practice of very long standing. Ways well known in one congregation may be unknown in a sister church. An established practice in a church may be no older than the memory of the oldest member. It may also be true that the rationale for a specific custom is lost in the dim past. The habits of any church can be very much like those of the members of a Roman Catholic church in northern Italy where parishioners genuflected faithfully before a blank wall without quite knowing why. Later, a restoration of the structure revealed a painting of the Madonna and Child which had been covered over with ordinary paint more than a century before. Only because of custom were the worshipers going through the motions of reverence.

It is time for us to look specifically at the possible functions of the deacon. We shall consider in this chapter the usual, more liturgical, responsibilities of the diaconate, and then move in subsequent chapters to some of the ministries which are possible within the freedom that exists in Christ, where service and witness are of primary importance. Deacons may truly become servants of the church and the world as they enter into some of these new ministries.

Baptism

Baptists tend to feel secure when the subject of baptism is discussed. Baptist churches are generally noted for this rite and frequently immersion is required before membership. They are surprised, therefore, when friendly critics within other parts of the Christian family tell them that their voice is muted concerning this distinctive witness because they have become lazy in their thinking about the meaning of their own ordinances. There does appear to be some truth to the charge that where baptism by immersion is a requirement for membership too little time is given to illuminating its significance. Perhaps deacons should find opportunity to keep their understanding of this ordinance fresh and vital by following the pastor in a careful study of this theme.[2]

We cannot here review the lengthy discussion which has gathered about baptism over the centuries. But our failure to try to understand it may permit us to treat sacred things perfunctorily, to interpret them erroneously, and to be silent when we should bear witness.

The early Christians clearly practiced baptism. It appears to have been inconceivable to them that Christians should not be baptized. This was no new rite to them, knowing as they did of the use of immersion in some of the ancient religions and among the Jews; but they burst it open with new mean-

[2] "Dominical ordinances" is a term which is often used to refer to baptism and the Lord's Supper as rites established, ordained by the Lord (Latin, *dominus*). Protestants hold to two ordinances in contrast to the seven sacraments of the Roman Catholic Church. Both "sacrament" and "ordinance" are often defined as the "outward and visible sign of an invisible grace." Protestants emphasize the ordinances as symbols or signs, and Baptists outside the United States freely use the term "sacrament" within this definition. The Catholic, for his part, believes that sacraments "contain and confer" grace by a virtue inherent in themselves but not apart from the attitude and intention of the recipient and administrant.

ing. In the classical statement of Romans 6:1-12, baptism is said to picture our oneness with Christ in his death and resurrection. It is an affirmation of faith that the believer unites himself with Christ so that his former life is crucified and buried with Christ and he rises with him to walk in newness of life (cf. Ephesians 4:20-24). It is a vivid portrayal of this aligning of life with Christ and the people of God. The rite takes on its meaning from God's redemptive act in Christ, the effectiveness and power of which are available to men today.

Perhaps, as some insist, we should think of baptism as a means of grace, since it holds before us the death of Christ, his burial, and resurrection in a way that calls for reverence and response. And it is certain that obedience to the ordinance of Christ is not without its blessing to the one baptized and to the congregation which sees this dramatic reminder of redemption, washing, separation unto Christ, and embodiment in the whole people of God (see Romans 6:1-11; Acts 22:16; Matthew 28:18-20; 1 Corinthians 12:13).

We often compare our baptism with that of Jesus, and one gets the feeling of walking in sacred places when he studies the baptism of our Lord – so unlike our baptism in that he was without sin, yet like our baptism in its portrayal of obedience to the Father and self-identification with the people (see Matthew 3:1-17; Mark 1:1-11; Luke 3:1-22). Jesus went to the banks of the Jordan, where men were publicly expressing their repentance and turning to the purposes of God under the ministry of John the Baptizer. By his own submission to this rite, our Lord took his stand with those who were renouncing any other bondage – to self, culture, class, or race – than to the will of God, thus joining his life to the life of the believing and obedient community of faith.

Another line of thought sees the baptism of Jesus as a prophetic act by which he pointed forward to the day when he would fulfill all righteousness by his self-giving on the cross.

For our part we look back to this same act in order to appropriate it as an event for us under the grace of the One who was dead and is living.

Careless administration of this ordinance and thoughtless submission to it will be impossible if one remembers what it signifies in the life of the church and for the candidate. One task of the diaconate is to fill the rite of baptism as full of meaning as possible, yet to maintain the stark simplicity which will make it the dramatic testimony to the act of Christ and the obedient faith of the candidate that it ought to be. It is a serious moment when one hears the minister say, "I baptize thee in the name of the Father, and of the Son, and of the Holy Spirit."

One distinctive belief about baptism through the years is that it is an act of responsible witness and obedience on the part of the Christian. One's relation to Jesus Christ is a personal choice and commitment, the results of which cannot be confessed in any way that denies to a person the joy and privilege of accepting for himself the reconciliation which God offers him in Christ. This emphasis on believers' baptism, even more than the mere practice of immersion, has been a basic Baptist conviction.

To emphasize the joining of faith and action means that the candidate for baptism is usually a responsible young person or adult who is sensitive to what is taking place. There is, therefore, a necessary preparation for baptism that is both spiritual and physical. If this rite is a sign of, and a witness to, one's identification with Jesus Christ as Savior and Lord, the candidate should have the clearest possible knowledge of what he is doing. Many pastors share their understanding of baptism by means of classes or individual instruction assisted by the deacons.

There is also a physical preparation for baptism that tries to anticipate and remove elements that might embarrass the candidate or distract his attention from the sacred matters at hand. To do this, instruction should be given him at the baptistry before the day of the service concerning how he enters the waters, where he turns, how he leaves the baptistry, and the way he takes to the dressing rooms. Provision will be made to screen the candidate as he leaves the waters. The deacons will want to be certain that the baptistry is cleaned and properly filled and that suitable, preferably private, dressing facilities are available. Most churches now use baptismal robes of different sizes in an opaque material, and some ask the deaconesses to baste in seams and pin up hems so every candidate is properly fitted. Needless to say, robes should be in good repair, clean, and pressed for the next use. When such careful attention is given to all of the details, the service will be more meaningful to all who share in it.

As the candidates are waiting to enter the waters of baptism, it is entirely fitting for a member of the diaconate to lead in a simple invocation of the presence of Christ in this significant event. Then, by making certain that the candidates enter the water at the right time, and by discreetly helping when needed, the deacon will give them a sense of security as they face this new experience, an experience of commitment, obedience, and witness. In this the deacon will be carrying on a very ancient tradition.

The Lord's Supper

We are in the long line of those Christians in every age who have found the high point of their worship in the Lord's Supper (called by many "the Eucharist" or thanksgiving). Unlike the Roman Catholics, we do not consider our celebration of the Supper a repetition of the sacrifice of Christ by which his grace becomes operative in the believing participant; rather we do view this as a time when, in memory and imagination, his death is brought before us anew, a time when he is present with his people and when we should be most sensitive to the mighty acts of God.[3]

Our commemoration of the Supper springs from that night when our Lord looked forward to his cross and to the continuing fellowship which would center upon the remembrance of his saving act (see Matthew 26:17-30; Mark 14:12-26; Luke 22:7-22; 1 Corinthians 11:23-26). The sacred-meal remembrance continued in the breaking of bread among the early disciples, on into the early church, and on to our own day.

The Supper brings together people of all sorts who, transcending all kinds of differences, gather for the purpose of worshiping and meeting anew the crucified but living Christ. The people's very being together by the act of Christ proclaims that God offers his grace to all, that he makes possible a redemptive reconciliation both between God and man and among men.

As they share in taking the symbols of Christ's suffering, Christians find each other through a communion in and with Christ. This very simple but dramatic ordinance, pointing as it does to Christ and his saving deed, speaks to Christian and non-Christian alike. It calls for a response in faith and obedience; it calls for wonder and awe; it points to the day of the ultimate victory of our Lord (see 1 Corinthians 11:26).

A perfunctory, slipshod observance of the Lord's Supper is

[3] The ordinances have often been referred to as "merely symbols." The fact is, we cannot live without symbols, whether it be the word that communicates, the caress of love, or the look of hate. Clothing can be a symbol of poverty, affluence, or taste. Symbols vary in power and usefulness, according to meanings and values that cluster around them, because of what they represent. The Lord's Supper can have, and should have, the power to *re-present* the cross to us and to our generation. It is something more than a series of ritual acts when it points beyond the elements, that is, the bread and the cup, to the body and blood of the Son of God given on Calvary.

inexcusable. Its preparation and reenactment should be given careful thought and planning.

The elements of the Supper are usually prepared on the evening before or early on the day of the observance and placed on the communion table.[4] The bread is covered by clean, white cloths, and lids are put over the trays containing the glasses. Frequently, a clean, freshly pressed cloth covers the whole table. A few churches follow the pattern of the Orthodox Church in having the elements brought forward by a family or group in the church as an offering, to serve as a reminder that we offer ourselves afresh whenever we remember our Lord's offering of himself.

The elements [5] have constantly been the center of discussion by churchmen. Opinions have varied as to whether the bread should be leavened or unleavened, specially prepared or the ordinary loaf from the table; and as to whether the cup should be served in individual containers or in the common chalice, and whether grape juice is as valid as wine. Such discussions seem to miss the vital issue, which is to ask whether the elements and the Supper minister to the memory, the imagination, and the will of the participants in such a way that faith is enriched and obedience strengthened.

A service in which simple things like bread and juice and physical actions are supposed to bring a message from God

[4] Protestants have considered the altar out of place in their churches because of the connotation of sacrifice which surrounds it in the Catholic Church. The Reformers pulled the altars away from the back walls of the chancels and treated them as tables where Christians gathered in communion with Christ and each other.

[5] The word "elements" is used to refer to the bread and cup used in the Lord's Supper. The word was used in late Latin for articles of food and drink. In earlier days of the church the word referred to the material substance of bread and wine which, when joined with the Word, became representative of Christ in his sacrifice.

to a gathered people is never to be taken lightly. The pastor and the diaconate will want to work out together the arrangement of the elements on the table, the seating of the deacons, and the way the congregation will be served. Everything possible should be done to convey the concept that the Lord's Supper is a message of God to man and that it involves a people who are in fellowship with Christ and with each other. Even such a minor thing as moving the trays and cups to a secluded place for cleaning and for disposal of the surplus may indicate our sensitivity to the feelings of others and our own sense of the fitness of things.

Every church edifice imposes certain limitations on the congregation. Some pastors conduct the service from the lectern and pulpit in the usual manner and move to the table only at the beginning of the communion service. Even though this may be a grudging concession to the design and acoustical properties of the sanctuary, it does maintain some resemblance to the ancient divisions of the "liturgy of the catechumens" and the "liturgy of the faithful," or the ante-communion and the communion. Other pastors conduct the entire service facing the congregation from behind the communion table in what is called "the basilican position."

This latter position is sometimes taken to emphasize the oneness of the people of God within which there may be differing functions but not differing positions before God. In this quest for a symbol of family unity few churches can go as far as one Reformed church in Europe which designed the sanctuary so that a table could be placed both across the entire front and down the length of the center aisle. All the communicants present are gathered at the table of the Lord. A few congregations have planned the seating in their new buildings in a circle with the table and pulpit in the center or on three sides of a chancel that juts out into the room.

Others have the deacons face the congregation with the pastor, and a few extend the seating of the deacons to join that of the congregation.

The deacons and pastor might profitably discuss the implications of the New Testament teaching of the unity of the body of Christ. How can the communion be planned to emphasize that this is not two or three orders of people but one family sharing the Lord's table and the Word? How can the diaconate and the pastor actually join their worship to that of the people when they have so many details on their minds? How best can the oneness of the church be held before the sick and shut-in as several deacons represent the larger congregation in communion in the sick room, nursing home, or hospital?

We need to ask if there is a place in the larger church for communion to be served in a home to people living in a given area, because there is ample proof that a person can relate well to only a very limited number of people. Some Anglican and Lutheran pastors abroad have found communion in the home (properly ordered, of course) a means of deepening Christian understanding and fellowship.

There are many who think it to be improper to take the communion service into the home or the sick room because it is an ordinance of the church. To others, however, this view seems to confine the idea of the church to a building or a special hour in the week, rather than to conceive of it as the people of God wherever and whenever they gather in the name of Christ. Let us grant that the communion is not to be lightly used at the whim of an individual or a group. For the sake of good order, the recognition of the congregation or the diaconate should be sought for any observance of the Supper. Communion is valid whenever Christians thoughtfully celebrate their salvation through Christ's self giving on the cross.

The Deacons' Fund

Tied closely to the Lord's Supper is the tradition of the deacons' fund which may trace its origins to the stories in the Acts of the Apostles when even Paul was pressed into service as courier to hurry the gifts of concerned Christians to the needy of Jerusalem. This may well be the first instance on record of people giving for the relief of folk whom they did not even know in another part of the world. In his *First Apology,* Justin Martyr said:

> What is collected is deposited with the president, and he takes care of orphans and widows, and those who are in want on account of sickness or any other cause, and those who are in bonds, and the strangers who are sojourners among us, and, briefly, he is the protector of all those in need.[6]

From these examples we can infer that the people of God cannot refuse to minister to the limits of their ability and without regard to possible returns.

Customarily the gifts for the deacons' fund are received just before the supper in token of our self giving, in gratitude for the good things of our common life, and in praise for the self offering of our Lord. Some churches assign a percentage of the regular giving of the congregation to the deacons' fund. This may be good if it makes possible an increase in the range of ministry without bypassing the instructional benefits which are gleaned from the proper use of a special offering.

Possibly the most common concern, and worthy of discussion by the deacons, is the question of how the deacons' fund can be administered without embarrassing the recipient of aid while at the same time providing an accounting to the church. Perhaps the problem can be met by placing the deacons' fund

[6] Cyril Richardson, ed., *Early Christian Fathers* in *The Library of Christian Classics* (Philadelphia: The Westminster Press, 1953), Vol. I, p. 287.

under the care of two or three of the deacons and the pastor. Any two of the committee may be given the power to evaluate the need and determine the aid to be given according to their best judgment. The treasurer of the deacons' fund may be authorized to forward funds immediately and to keep the records of income and expenditure with meticulous care. Code numbers can be used in public reports referring to those receiving aid.

The recipient of aid should never be made to feel that he is receiving charity. His need is a matter of family concern within the congregation. There are some who will want to work out a plan for repayment, and their wish should be honored, but there are others who can never hope to pay back the smallest sum. Help should be given for the love of Christ, not for hope of return.

Every effort should be made to remove the causes of need as well as to deal with the immediate need itself. Some churches, for example, have drawn on experienced individuals in the congregation to give instruction to people who do not possess a rudimentary knowledge of the value of money and the ways to manage it. One church became aware of a sharp increase in the number of needy families because an industry with a long history in the town had been defeated by progress. Its boards joined to spark what proved to be a fruitful search for new industry with new jobs to give aid and a sense of dignity and worth to people in the town.

The enormous problems of our mass society have compelled the creation of complex structures by which city, state, and federal agencies have taken over many of the "caring activities" which once belonged to the Christian conscience. This has led some to ask if the deacons' fund is an anachronism. But the issues must be kept in sharp focus. This kind of aid for human need is imperative even though we may not like it. The problems confronting us by such things as the rats in our cities, starvation in our slums, care for the aged and crippled, and the training of the retarded, are too pervasive and complex to be met by means that were adequate in our early agrarian society. More massive action is imperative and is often available, but in spite of all that the public agencies can do, our involvement is still needed in the catastrophic situations and desperate needs all about us that spill over the boundaries of established programs. The Christian will try to overcome the impersonal dealings that are part of even the most sensitive of our huge programs by means of simple kindness and Christian concern. But any suggestion of competition with public and quasi-public agencies should be avoided.

In the complexity of modern social welfare organizations, the church is tempted to withdraw from many legitimate needs, in contrast to the day when pressing human needs were visible at every doorstep. It should be the task of the diaconate to reinvolve the church in the burdens of individuals and groups today. Some church groups have adopted nursing homes as centers for their concern; others serve the needs of retarded children, or assist in job training and Head Start programs and a host of other efforts currently being made to help persons. Perhaps subsidy from the deacons' fund is a valid expression of Christian compassion if it can free members of the congregation to answer the insistent call of human agony.

In spite of all the creativity and sensitivity the diaconate can muster, there are those who will question motives and criticize what is done and the way in which it is done. Nothing, however, should swerve the deacons from their mandate to serve and assist those who are in need to sense the love and care of God through his people. The deacons' fund is an extension of the interest and concern which the members of the congregation should be expressing every day in their personal and corporate experience. Jesus' statement ". . . as you did it to one of the least of these my brethren, you did it to me" (Matthew 25:40) is a challenge for his people to meet him in the persons of the needy wherever they may be and whatever their burden.

Concern for the Word

The deacon's responsibility for the ministry of the Word finds expression in several ways. For example, a vacancy in the pastorate is the occasion for forming a pulpit committee to expedite the search for someone to fill the pastoral office. The diaconate is usually represented on such a committee if, indeed, it does not actually become the pulpit committee, as happens in a few instances. The more accepted practice is to have a committee which is widely representative of the boards, major committees, and organizations of the church. The committee usually requests the executive minister from the city or state office to work together in drawing up a profile of the present and future needs of the congregation as well as a profile of the kind of minister who might give the congregation creative leadership. He will, then, recommend several carefully chosen men who may be interviewed, and he will guide the committee in the etiquette of calling a minister. The executive minister is most anxious to help both minister and congregation to deal with major issues as they try to learn more about each other in the light of a task to be shared.

The deacon's role is to share in stating the inner needs of the congregation and the objectives in ministry which the committee must keep in mind as a pastor is sought. Both the committee and the prospective pastor must be scrupulously honest about their needs, their expectations of each other, and the dreams they project into the future until both can agree that God has brought them together.

Beyond aiding in the search for a pastor, the deacons are

frequently given the responsibility for choosing the persons who will supply the pulpit in times of illness or vacation leave. State and city denominational offices, seminaries, and college departments of religion can often suggest qualified persons who can enter into the ministry of the Word. The chairman of the diaconate should contact promptly the person chosen to be the guest minister in order to gain his acceptance and to acquaint him with the hours of service and his responsibilities. A conversation by phone should be followed by a letter of confirmation giving directions to the church, naming the person who will meet the guest, the portions of the service he will carry, and the honorarium.

It is a simple matter, though often overlooked, for a deacon to meet a guest speaker on his arrival at the church to review the order of service and come to a clear agreement on who will be responsible for its various parts. Also often overlooked is the preparation for the introduction of a guest speaker, an introduction which should be factual, concise, and expressive of Christian warmth.

Many churches have the diaconate to lead certain midweek services, not that they might compete with the pastor in the preparation and delivery of sermons, but to bear witness to their own understanding of the ways of God with men. This custom, wisely used, can permit the voice of the thoughtful laity to be heard. To strengthen further the witness of the laity, ministers may involve the deacons in searching out the deeper needs of the people to which they can address their ministries.

Some ministers have asked the diaconate to help choose sermon themes or even to react to sermons that were yet to be preached. It is understandable that few pastors have moved in this direction. There is a natural fear that the freedom of the pulpit may be compromised. Evidence abounds in both the Old and New Testaments, and in church history, that the voice of God can be stifled when the pulpit is not free. Every congregation needs to be called beyond where it is, a call that will not be heard if dialogue with the minister is used to shackle him rather than make his ministry vital to the congregation and the community. One insightful deacon urged his pastor to enter a program of continuing education because, as he said, "You have been here four years and we have chipped off your rough corners. You are too much like us to help us in our development."

Joint exploration, by the diaconate and the pastor, of the needs which call for prayer, service, and witness can be one forward step a church can take immediately. This kind of dialogue can clarify the preacher's thinking in the light of the specific needs he knows, and it can challenge the diaconate to develop their own deepest Christian thought.

For Further Consideration

1. How do you understand baptism and the Lord's Supper in their significance to the church? How can their observance be enriched in your church?
2. Is the use of the deacons' fund an extension of the interest and concern which the members of the congregation should be expressing every day?
3. What does it mean for the diaconate to have a concern for the Word?

THE DEACON AND THE PEOPLE

Words such as care, concern, service, and ministry have run through these chapters in a constant refrain. The example of Christ and his call are sufficient authority for this. Working after the pattern of our Lord, the diaconate and all other church leaders are to bring to fuller maturity the relations among believers and between all men and their Lord, as well as to help Christians develop in their ministry in the world.

The Fellowship

Care for the membership is a primary consideration for the diaconate. We are members one of another and are pledged to share our burdens and our joy in Christ. It is to be hoped that this unity, this coherence of the group, can be a witness to the outsider as well as a service to the insider. The message which the church *lives* is frequently better understood by the non-member than its declarations: By this message men most readily evaluate the gospel.

Hopefully the fellowship of Christians will be a sign in the world pointing to the love of God for man and testifying to the reconciling and renewing power of the gospel in the whole range of human experience. This sign alone gives point to a genuine diaconal concern for the quality and richness of the congregational life. There are many ways to work at this both by the personal effort of the individual deacon and by the involvement of groups of Christians.

For example, the deacon traditionally has been supportive of the people. There will always be those of the fellowship who need some tangible evidence of God's loving care through his people, perhaps because of pain, loneliness, personal need, or the events of that fateful day when the skies fall in.

Every ministry calls particular skills into play. The deacon will be well repaid if he develops and refines the expression of his innate concern and gifts by study with the pastor. And, by the example of their own activities, the members of the board of deacons can lead the congregation to an awareness of the ministry Christians should have to each other.

The deacon has been committed as well to the spiritual growth of each person. One popular program is the "Sector Zone Plan" which divides the membership and community into small geographical units with a deacon assigned to each area. Variations of the plan have been used to promote the budget program, or to form study groups, therapy groups, or other groups that draw persons into Christian relationship. But the diaconate will recall that while one may have many acquaintances, he is able to share life at a deeper level with very few people. He will view the "Sector Zone Plan" as a means to bring people together in more intimate groups, wherein one large congregation becomes a cluster of small congregations for the sake of a kind of Christian fellowship which runs deeper than a coffee-and-doughnuts sociability. By recognizing the need for Christians to find each other, the deacons can lead the church in its ministry to diverse people who live out their lives in different contexts even though they are members of the same congregation.

Yet another example of care is found in the churches that use records imaginatively. One church requested a semi-invalid to tabulate the registration cards which were filled out by members and visitors alike every Sunday. She could see real people behind these cards, and she frequently reminded the deacons that contact was being lost with a family, a student, or a young married couple. Quite a few persons were not forgotten because she helped a concerned diaconate to remember.

Unfortunately, there are some who absent themselves from the worship and work of the people of God for extended periods of time. Everyone wants to avoid legalism, but it is not honest to let the lapsed or careless member assume that all is well. A review of the membership rolls will reveal where calls should be made by the deacons. Where sincere and repeated efforts at recovery fail, a series of letters can plead in turn for recovery and renewal, state the requirements of church membership, and, finally, recall the constitutional requirements for dismissal. When all else has failed, steps should be taken for dismissal. Needless to say, this dismissal is based on broken fellowship rather than lessened financial support.

An increasing number of deacons are seeing the value of an every-member canvass that has nothing to do with money, in which visitors are trained to go out, frequently with a deacon, to serve as they think best in every home. They express the interest of the congregation in each member, interpret the mission of the church, and draw out the dreams people have for their church and their own ministry. Often when some deeper need rises to the surface, the visitors are able to give help and support to a fellow Christian in a time of testing.

The concern of the diaconate for the member does not end when people move from the community. By personal contact before moving day, by letters to them at their new address, by letters to a pastor who may serve them in their new community, the diaconate can assist mobile Christians in maintaining some stability in their Christian faith and some maturity in their witness.

The deacons should assist others in finding their ministry. As leaders of the church in its care for people, the diaconate works with different groups. The members of one board who took their registration cards seriously noticed a new group of people in the community and among the visitors. In this case the group consisted of retired people. The deacons moved to meet the changing situation creatively by drawing on members of the congregation for a basic organization, for program assistance, and services. Groups for study, recreation, fellowship, travel, and services were soon helping older persons to have a sense of worth in meaningful relationships and usefulness.

It is obvious that the deacons must draw upon other individuals and groups in the church to provide supportive relationships and mutual help among the people. Only as their concern pervades each group in the church and church school can the ministry be fulfilled. We cannot do without the example of board members, but examples alone may not be sufficient. One board decided that each group in the congregation needed to evaluate its own life. A questionnaire to every organization of the church was devised and filled out at the annual workers' retreat. Thorny questions were asked about the outreach of the group, the growth and ministry of its members, and its watchcare program. One group decided it was not fulfilling its stated purpose and took needed action.

The day has not yet come when we should react against the modern emphasis on the small group. The wise diaconate will see many ministries which may be accomplished through them, either in groups already established or in the formation of others for a specific time and purpose. They give the alert church an insight into the actual problems which people face, and they carry the witness of faith nearer to the place where people have their deepest experiences. They certainly provide a more intimate life together in Christ than is possible in the eleven o'clock preaching service.

Fellowship does not become vital by means of trivialities; it does not just happen. It comes from sharing life at its depths. Groups make this possible in our world of estrangement and isolation when persons find common concerns at some focal points, whether in the ordinary places like the choir, the circle, the class, the committee meeting, or in the unusual spot such as care for the aged, nurture of the unusual child, a Head Start program, or some special mission. The appropriate center around which meaningful Christian groups will take shape can be decided only as each case presents itself; it cannot be predetermined.

Yet the deacons have some very serious questions to ask even as they encourage persons to find relationships in groups. For example: "When people buy privacy in the form of apartments, fenced yards, and country houses, is it wise on the part of the church to impel them into unwanted relationships, or should a way be found to encourage a redemptive quality in those ties which they now have?" "Do people in ghettoes and overcrowded housing developments need more togetherness or a new quality of relationships?"

It must also be asked how meaningful relationships can be built between people in the same congregation when they do not know each other, are not related, do not work or play together, and may not even live in the same community? Can people be alerted to the common human need for a life with others? How can a cross section of humanity be helped to feel a oneness in their humanity and in Christ? Is it possible to have unity with diversity, or must we forever continue to fall into our separate categories of race, age, possessions, education, and what have you?

Let us not interpret this emphasis on group work to mean that there is no longer any reason for the diaconate to be concerned for corporate public worship. The value of the small group has been stressed not because it is the only way to serve needs but because it is a method which has been subject to notable oversight in the life of the church. Actually the deacons should see corporate worship as a necessary ingredient of the Christian's life and fellowship.

What God has done, is doing, and will be doing through the larger fellowship should be celebrated by that larger fellowship in the house of God. The ordinances serve to remind us of our common bonds in the saving act of Christ. Even though faith is a very personal thing, it incorporates the believers into a larger fellowship; and it is to the church of his creation that God has given his gifts. The debilitating effect of solitariness will soon take over in the lives of Christians when they do not gather to recall the acts of God on their behalf and the purposes to which he calls them.

There is a link between a deeply significant corporate worship and the health of the Christian community. Some pastors review the order and the materials of worship periodically with the diaconate. Changes in forms are introduced gradually from time to time to be certain that the statement of the gospel is addressed to current needs in life and that the response of the people in praise and obedience is related to contemporary issues. By sharing in rather intensive studies of worship, its history, structures, and materials, the pastor and the diaconate may be able to shape a worship service that will be more meaningful for all who share in it.

The New Member

Many persons experience difficulty in finding their way in their new-found faith. The care of the new member falls quite naturally under the responsibilities of the diaconate.

Most churches have designated the diaconate, or a subcommittee of it, to serve as a membership committee. This places the deacons in the position of being the first official group to meet the new member, whether he comes by profession of faith and baptism, by transfer of letter, or by renewal of Christian commitment. Serious thought should be given to the procedure to follow.

The diaconate will want to learn about the Christian experience and background of the new member both through carefully phrased conversation and the use of one of the many forms of checklist now available from denominational presses. It might be well for a committee to draw up its own questionnaire, using the checklist principle but adding questions about family ties, schools attended, employment, and involvements in the community as a means of learning where the members of the congregation are bearing their primary witness.

The deacons who are experienced in the Christian faith may need a word of caution against several tendencies in the matter of interrogating the candidate. The first is an inclination toward expecting a candidate to give an expression of faith that is identical with their own, whereas they should know that God works with each one as a person, and that few people have the same experience. The second is a desire to hear a new Christian say more than he presently understands about the Christian faith. Third, and closely related, is the expectation that a younger person will have the experiences, understanding, and vocabulary of adults, and that unless he does so his experience is not valid. A fourth tendency, because of the nature of the meeting, is to impress the new person with cold formality and cheerless interrogation rather than personal interest and joy in a commonly held faith. Then, finally, membership committees frequently prod the new member into talking while they refrain from sharing their own experiences of Christ and his church in a word of praise, testimony, or instruction.

One step more is essential, namely, to ask about the aspirations of the new member as he enters the fellowship. He may have a vision, a zeal, a devotion that should be recognized when the deacons begin to help others discover their own areas of ministry. One church found a kindergarten teacher who had never served in the church because she was not asked about her skills and concerns. Another person, a banker, refused to be made a treasurer because his deeper interest was to serve Christ with the dedicated gifts of an unusually fine musician. Others professed Christian concerns that were best fulfilled in ministries extending beyond the church walls.

The deacons should be interested in the Christian education of the new member. Some boards sponsor instructional groups themselves while others assist the Christian education department to formulate an effective program of membership classes. Many churches now insist that every new member study in discipleship classes, whether he is a young believer or a mature, experienced Christian. This plan is particularly valid where the classes offer the beginnings of new relationships in the congregation and where the courses stress the unique ties and ministries characterizing the local church. The classes should be arranged with sufficient frequency that incoming members can become involved at a time when new decisions and enthusiasms are still fresh and vital. But the deacons should take a continuing interest in the classes, arranging for the sessions, encouraging attendance, and reviewing the effectiveness of the program, picking up the details of registration, sending reminders, and providing materials.

There is no uniform pattern for the classes. They are held at different times of the week and for differing lengths of time. Common patterns call for six to eight, or even twelve sessions. In any event, the curriculum reviews the biblical teaching concerning the Christian faith and the church, the Christian's missionary responsibilities, and the denominational and interdenominational ties the church enjoys. Most religious book stores offer many fine curricular materials for this purpose. Many ministers covet this type of setting for themselves in order to become acquainted with new members and to share in developing their understanding of the Christian faith. This plan does not preclude the use of other members in positions of leadership.

Diaconal concerns should find expressions as each new member is integrated into the fellowship. Few people find it simple to move into the circles of church life and ministry. By assigning a member of the diaconate to each new member as friend, counselor, and guide for six months to a year, new and often deep relationships can be established, and pastoral care becomes a reality.

By whatever name the plan is called, the purpose is to exercise a degree of helpful watchcare until the member is a vital part of the learning, serving, and witnessing community. This concern is in a spiritual succession to the ministry which the risen Christ gave Paul when he urged that those who had received forgiveness be given ". . . a place among those who are sanctified by faith in me" (Acts 26:18). The purposes of the church in its evangelistic outreach are not fulfilled until the new member is an integral part of the Christian family. There is no fulfillment for any of us as long as areas of our lives remain closed to the rule of Christ.

The Witness

The diaconate should give active leadership in the outreach of the church, either in primary leadership if so designated by the church, or in a supportive role if another committee has been given the leadership in evangelism. For our discussion we shall assume that this responsibility is given to the whole diaconate or a subcommittee of the board.

Several basic facts should be kept in mind by the deacon. The first fact is that evangelism is the privilege of all Christians, not of the clergy only, nor of the diaconate only. Every person bears a positive or negative witness to the gospel. As a layman he does not need to struggle to shape contacts with the non-Christian because he is in the world every day. He is already at the center of discussion, making policy-shaping decisions and opinion-forming activities. The major question is how his witness in his world can be enriched in the direction of a positive ministry.

Secondly, few, if any, of the members who are new to a church in a given year have come from stark unbelief to faith by the witness of the church. Christians so readily worship with each other, meet each other, and judge the world and others by their own kind that the millions in our own country who have never had ten minutes of Christian training in their lives are forgotten. Because of either our self-centeredness or our simple timidity, we deprive many of these of the opportunity to see the love of God epitomized in the intelligent, genuine concern of Christian people. We simply must work at finding ways to get near people and to get their attention for the gospel.

Thirdly, the modern movement to a staff ministry has invited the laity to shift their responsibilities onto the shoulders of professionals, thereby robbing lay people of opportunities to develop deeper understandings and sharpened competencies in their own life and witness. We forget that Christianity spread across the ancient world with incredible speed because shopkeepers and soldiers, domestic servants and craftsmen, merchants and refugees ministered, each according to his opportunity and ability. We need to recover the vision of a lay witness today.

Effective evangelistic witness involves preparation for both informal witness by the individual and the more formal and structured methods of the church. The informal witness is carried out by one's mode of life, his Christian sensitivity in the daily round with family and friends, at work and in recreation. True witness is life lived with others and the word of testimony and faith given at the right time.

The more structured witness of the people of God builds heavily on the quality of the fellowship which is obvious to the world, the accumulated effectiveness of individual lives devoted to Christ, and the concerned personal and corporate involvement of the Christian community in the issues of our times. Both forms of witness demand preparation.

The deacons should lead in a preparation of the people which goes beyond the strengthening of the fellowship, mentioned previously. Hopefully, members of the diaconate will keep alive their own understanding of the Christian message. Then by means of schools of evangelism, suggested readings, or special classes they can draw the congregation into serious thought about basic Christian doctrines concerning human need and sin, the divine love and grace, the nature of decision, and the Christian life.

Basic studies in the church should not be made more simple than their importance warrants. The rising educational standards of the people and the tremendous interest in adult courses offered by secular institutions indicate that the church should take lay education more seriously.

There is also a preparation that helps the church to know what it should do. One essential is to keep track of those for whom the church should assume responsibility. The alert diaconate will have little trouble creating a file that will provide such information as name, address, phone number, family, occupation, and other information that will be helpful to staff or lay workers. No church will have any difficulty in finding a challenge at hand if friends and relatives of members, new residents in the community, and visitors in the church activities are thought of as being under the shepherd concern of the church.

Several ministers have followed the lead of a certain pastor who requested members of church groups to think of one or two persons who needed to know Christ and the ministry of the church. They were then challenged to indicate what their own ministry would be to the persons they had listed, and finally they worked out in detail how others in the congregation could help them in their ministry. In another place, a deacon and his wife became concerned about their neighbors. Each week they invited a few of them to their home to get acquainted and thereby expanded the responsibility of the whole church. There are, of course, the usual things to be done in building a responsibility file, but it is time to go beyond this if we are to break out of the circle of previously interested persons to serve the vast numbers who do not now walk with Christ.

If we can think beyond a mere interest in programs within the church, a part of our preparation for ministry is to know the areas of need which should be met and to hold these before congregations as challenges for ministry. More than one church has reshaped its youth program when it took seriously the way adult indifference to youth and adult exploitation of youth contribute to the sad story told by police and social work records. One church recognized the presence of minority groups in the community and opened doors to the gospel by caring enough to form classes in English, diet, finances, and homemaking. There is no reason why a church with an alert diaconate cannot discover more things to do than it can ever carry out. The imagination is staggered to think of the scope and immediacy of ministry that any congregation would face if the members went to every house in the average city block and asked in what ways the church could serve the people living there.

After preparation there should come ministry. We are "a chosen race, a royal priesthood, a holy nation, God's own people. . . ." (1 Peter 2:9) in order to declare the mighty acts of God. Among the free churches the evangelistic meeting has been one of the most common ways to reach men. The purpose is to bring to the church services those who should hear the gospel. Visiting missioners, or the pastor, may preach the Word of the gracious acts of God in Christ in the traditional manner, or they may use the dialogue sermon, drama, films, music, or some other less usual form of the communication arts.

Evangelistic outreach that takes the uncommitted seriously does not just happen. Weeks of planning go into deciding the type of effort to be carried out, securing the visiting missioner, if any, clearing the church calendar, preparing advertising, working out the program with the leader, and implementing any visitation which may be planned.

Accepting the reality that most non-Christians will not enter the church building, some boards are leaning toward other modes of evangelism. In the early nineteenth century, Thomas Chalmers, the Scottish pastor and professor, recovered a New Testament procedure which had become obscured by sacramentalism and an overdependence on the spoken word, namely, home visitation evangelism. Only in the second quarter of this century did its use spread through the churches until the visitation program now should be considered a normal part of the pastoral program. It takes many forms. It may refer to a house-by-house census as a forerunner to a systematic outreach, or to a hastily contrived means to recruit new members for the church records. At its best, however, it is a serious and sometimes costly effort to relate Christian people of the church to those for whom it is responsible.

The basic pattern is to organize teams of two persons to visit in homes to press the claims of Christ (see Mark 6:7-13; Luke 10:1-12). If a large number of workers is needed, a more complex structure is formed, with a captain for approximately every ten teams to assist in recruiting the callers, to process the calling lists from the responsibility file, assign the calls to visitors, and arrange for their attendance at several training sessions led by the pastor or visiting missioner.

By now it is obvious how essential a general chairman, often a deacon, is to any special evangelistic effort if no responsibility is to be ignored, no opportunity unclaimed. He will provide times of training and prayer for the visitors. He will recruit skilled persons to assist with publicity, to maintain the necessary records, to plan the follow-up ministries, and he will make every effort to rally the strength of the church around the program. In larger churches a number of members may be recruited to serve on subcommittees that will help to carry the heavy load of details, all working under the coordinating hand of a special chairman. But even in some large churches it may be necessary to begin this type of ministry with a small group of concerned people who will work closely with the pastor and deacons.

Training may take the form of lectures on Christian witnessing, but many persons have found that times of simple, informal sharing with their fellow-workers about their faith and life in the church serve to sharpen the content of their witness. Deep-seated convictions are brought into the forefront of their consciousness, and some of the many ways in which Christ meets persons become clear and aid them in meeting the needs of others.

Some churches, by using visitation to open up new relationships, try to reach that increasing host of folks who have had no serious contact with the church. Calls are made with the simple questions in mind: "How can we minister to these persons in the name of Christ? What continuing relationships can we of the church develop so the gospel of Christ can be seen as the living reality we say it is?" The attitudes engendered by this kind of primary commitment to ministry often remove barriers to the communication of the Christian faith, and the pressure for instant success is taken off the shoulders of the visitor. The long-term benefits are frequently amazing.

It might be well for the diaconate to discuss the nonverbal communication that takes place among Christians. Actions are easily read and understood. The nonverbal witness of friendship, caring, and involvement must frequently precede and undergird a verbal witness to the saving grace of Christ. Visitation in order just to be there, to become a part of the life, burdens, and joys of another, has enormous power to communicate the love and concern of Christ.

Whenever we of the church ask where and how we must minister, we face the fact that no one or two simple evangelistic procedures can meet the vast needs of our generation or express the manifold concerns of the congregation. We have a tendency to act as if there is but one way to make the gospel crystal clear to everyone, as if all concerns of the church can be funneled into one expression. A simple sharing with a few friends about the way each one decided to be a Christian will reveal that few, if any two, had similar experiences or were moved by the same mode of evangelism. Why, then, should we think that God will deal with others than as the quite individually unique beings they are?

The diaconate must ensure that the gospel goes where the people are, that it is released into the world to those who live in the glory and misery of modern existence. This is why new patterns of visitation are being used by some congregations. This is why there is a deep need for many approaches, often new approaches, to evangelism. We shall return to this in another context.

Enough has been said to indicate that these can be exciting days for a diaconate that leads a congregation by example, instruction, and counsel in an expression of its diaconal life, providing it moves out in positive, creative ways that affirm the work of the gospel. To challenge complacency, to assert the meaning of the gospel in its purposes for the church, can be a daring thing. Then to work at ways to express this challenge in life can call out the best thought, planning, and action we can muster. For the sake of people in our kind of world this needs to be done, and the deacon himself should be prepared devotionally, emotionally, and with understanding to give leadership for the days ahead. What may be involved in all this will engage our attention next.

For Further Consideration

1. What would be the best possible plans your church could adopt for the care of the fellowship?
2. How are new members integrated into the life of your church?
3. How best may the diaconate sensitize and prepare persons for a ministry of service and witnessing?
4. What forms of outreach does your church use? What new forms should be considered?

NEW DAYS: NEW PATHS

We are moving through strange new days. Miracles of transportation get us to any part of the globe in a matter of hours and they bring other races and nationalities to be our neighbors. It was never that way before. Even at home we are a mobile people, whether socially by education, position, or wealth, or geographically by personal, governmental, or corporate decision. The girl who attended twenty schools in twelve years of public education was a product of the mobility which now causes one family in five to move each year. Some pastors report that they serve in areas where the turnover in population ranges from 10 percent to almost 50 percent annually. They often testify as well to the emotional, moral, and spiritual price that people pay for their restless existence. We have not yet met this challenge adequately.

No generation of adults has ever spared its criticism of youth. It is easy enough to quarrel with a generation that gives us such visible products as beatniks, hippies, and yippies, plus other species yet to come, but time is moving on and the need for ministry is imperative.

While we push back the boundaries of space there are some dark curtains remaining to be pushed aside on our own planet. Minority groups have seen the rising promise that their lives and those of their children may be better. They are impatient for dreams to take on reality, and who can find fault with them for their hopes? Automation and computers have taken over many tasks, until some fear that human values are being lost in the whirring disks and tapes of sophisticated machines. Cities are erupting all over the landscape. Planners are beginning to ask what values should determine the future shape of our cities — automobiles, industries, schools, recreation spots, or persons. And need one mention that crime, war, greed, and noninvolvement are outrageous curtains that still need to be pulled back?

People are gathered up in every one of the issues of our day. In them they live out the glory and misery, the joy and sadness, the victory and defeat of our common life. And where people are, there must be also a ministry in the name of Christ. Unusual and dynamic ministries must be formed to make known the love of Christ in unusual and moving days.

The new day is not *out there some place.* We are squarely in it, and it has come into our congregation. These are not new words. Change has confronted the church repeatedly throughout its history, but now we are the ones who should know what the kaleidoscopic changes of our own days are bringing to both the world and the church itself.

The Church and Its Own Life

The church is not escaping the winds of change, and for the

diaconate to raise questions about its inner life or its ministry means that available data and resulting conclusions should be up to date. Two common assumptions are: (a) that drastic change rarely comes in a local church, and (b) that those who are at the heart of its life obviously know what is happening. Both assumptions are wrong. A sufficient number of churches have had their existence threatened by problems within the congregation to remind us that change often can be rapid and destructively traumatic. And some churches, looking back, can see where vital information that might have averted tragic failures was overlooked for months and even years by people who were on the scene. We can no longer afford to work at the ministries of the church on the basis of unresearched and highly emotional reactions.

Many factors in the internal life of the church should be known if the deacons are to serve effectively. Whether the necessary studies should be made annually or every few years at previously determined dates is a matter for the diaconate to decide. Also to be determined is whether skillful individuals or a special committee should be chosen to provide the necessary data to the deacons. The basic question is: "What kind of information can be helpful?" A complete reply cannot be given, for any reply varies with time, persons, and place; but some examples may help.

Since it is a fact that many people, particularly in urban areas, select their church home for reasons other than previous denominational ties, many pastors can say that they have numerous denominations represented in the membership. This fact can be read off the surface if one has only a casual acquaintance with a congregation. Rarely, however, will one find either a pastor or a diaconate in a position to say how many people have come from each denomination and what should be done in pastors' classes and individual meetings to help this group or that become one with their newly chosen, particular community of faith. This kind of diversity has often brought with it problems in Christian education, missionary giving, evangelism, worship patterns, and denominational affiliation, usually because available facts were not carefully analyzed and then matched with a plan to meet the needs of the various groups.

A few churches have been surprised at the insights which they have gained when simple studies were made of the age, sex, occupation, educational background, and economic levels of the church members. What is to be said when these figures are put alongside similar statistics from the community as a whole, and there is no correlation?

One church, located in a strongly industrialized, strongly labor-union neighborhood, should have asked questions about its ministry before an outsider reminded them that they did not have a union member in the congregation. Questions should be asked where the average age of the congregation is over sixty and that of the community is under forty-five, or where the church gears its program only to families when there is a high incidence of single persons of all ages in the community. Even a difference in educational levels between the church and the community can erect enormous barriers to worship and Christian education programs unless the diaconate gives serious thought to surmounting them. One frequently hears of a "women's church" but seldom has any such slant been permitted to affect the shaping of the church program for further outreach.

Available data should be looked at squarely, in order to create an awareness of facts about ministry. The information that provides a realistic view of the congregation is a prelude to effective planning.

A simple graph like that on the following page can give significant aid to understanding a church. Each square represents a person. The left half of the graph represents the male, and the right half the female portion of the study. The horizontal rows of squares represent age levels.

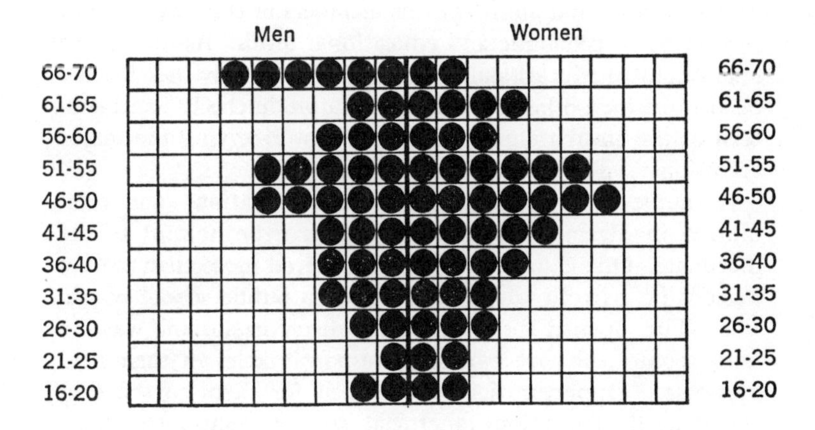

One church decided to evaluate its program of evangelism. When a graph was drawn up, it clearly showed that most of those engaged in all phases of the outreach program came from the older groups, and the women outnumbered the men. When a similiar graph of those who had entered the church in a five-year period proved to be roughly similar to that of those engaged in the outreach effort, the diaconate was in a position to think about broadening its base of workers in order to enlarge the boundaries of its outreach.

A set of similar graphs might help a church to discover weak places in its ministry. For example, a graph in which the horizontal bars represent age groupings might reveal over-emphasis on one or two age levels in the church. One in which the horizontal lines represent various church groups may indicate where fellowship needs to be strengthened, program enriched, or even leadership changed. Then, too, the diaconate should be very careful not to minister beneath the understanding and abilities of its members in this day of rapid upgrading of economic and educational levels. Assigning the horizontals to educational or economic levels may indicate the need to include other groupings of people in the life and concern of the church along with those now receiving the major attention.

A simple census of the occupations, avocations, and community involvements of the members can be helpful to the diaconate. One church suddenly discovered more than twenty persons on its rolls who were related to public school education. This opened the doors for ministry in specific ways to help people who face particular responsibilities in their field of service. Opportunities were shaped for them to share in clarifying their positions on crucial issues and supportive relationships were made available to those facing serious testing.

One pastor discovered the leading participants in the local power structures in the congregation he served. He did not tell them what to do, but he tried to enlarge their understanding of the Christian faith through classes and special fellowship groups and to support them when their convictions were put to the test.

It is not a simple matter to decide how well the church is caring for its own, but we must work at it. A few churches have developed simple questionnaires that help each organized group to determine to what degree it is fulfilling its ministry, the purposes that brought it into existence. Seldom is major surgery indicated, but each group must face up to the nature of its contributions to the welfare and ministry of the household of faith.

The Church in Its Community

The diaconate should lead in taking a long, hard look at its community. To say that few of the membership come from the immediate neighborhood is to confess a failure in mission. When one minister discovered that people around the corner from his church edifice could not direct strangers to its doors, he realized that there had been a serious failure in ministry.

There are those who maintain with some cogency that there is no such thing as a stable community. If that is even partially true, the diaconate should move toward a series of studies of the neighborhood spaced at intervals of two or three years. A bit of time dedicated by interested members to researching the area will hold before the church the changing profile of the community. Experienced and highly qualified assistance can be had from the national and area offices of the denomination or from the sociology department of a local college. City and county planning commissions have a wealth of pertinent information available and will even try to predict future trends. But the data is useless if it is not applied to the realities of ministry.

One congregation erected a new edifice. In a short time it was separated from the people by a new freeway that the planning commission had known about for years. A little investigation would have saved enormous disappointment and investment. There was another congregation that thought it could never gain strength because no one stayed around very long, but a city planner knew that the average resident in that area lived in his home for fifteen years.

Members of another church were convinced that the future was bleak because 87 percent of the population was of another faith. They had not made new studies, and times had changed. A very simple investigation revealed that adherents of the once-predominant faith were now actually a very small minority of the population. The new mission field of the church was to be found in the 47 percent of the population of all ages who were single.

Two churches in separate cities heard, the one from a denominational worker and the other from a planning commission worker, that they faced a future rapid change in the ethnic composition of their neighborhoods. Appearances contradicted the reports, but one church took the matter seriously by adjusting its ministry while the other ignored the prediction. Today the one church continues to minister, in quite different ways to be sure, and the other one has ceased to exist.

Police, school, and social-work officials can frequently point to areas in which a Christian ministry is needed. This may be with youth, among alcoholics, or on behalf of the culturally deprived. Frequently such leaders can point to more individuals and groups that need help than any one church can effectively serve. A system of priorities must then be developed on the basis of meeting the most imperative needs the resources at hand will permit.

Sometimes nonscientific methods will point to the avenue for service. A group of men in casual conversation came to the realization that not a business in the whole area was home-owned. Following this clue they investigated further and concluded that no power structure existed on behalf of the area that might care about the quality of schooling, the character of the housing, the availability of suitable recreation, and the welfare of the persons living there. Sensing a vacuum of leadership which could lead to a deterioration of the district with its inevitable damage to persons and to the Christian witness, they promoted a series of programs in the church to help create a sense of community among the residents.

Several congregations in the mountain states were led to spend an hour in small groups discussing just two questions: (a) What are the greatest moral and spiritual problems in our city? and (b) What should we do about them as Christians? In an amazing way both the open wounds and the deeply buried, festering sores were pointed up when the people shared their knowledge of their city. Naturally any information gathered so informally must be checked carefully. If verified, the diaconate should be ready to give long hours to considering what such facts may say about the development of the church program.

An increasing number of churches have incontrovertible proof that their apparently effective youth programs are not reaching those who have never heard the gospel. One church verified rumors of an astounding amount of immorality among students of high school age. The church's members confessed their failure and then set about finding ways to establish communication with a whole generation of young people.

There exist a host of issues in any community which clamor for the Christian fellowship to investigate, analyze in the light of the gospel, and then plan for effective action. The diaconate could well be involved, since their humanity binds them to every man tangled in the web of life, and their continuing Christian commitment is ". . . to serve and bear witness . . ." (Acts 26:16) in the name of Christ.

The Deacons and the Renewal of Worship

As we have seen earlier, the deacons have been involved in worship throughout the centuries. Usually, however, they have acted as assistants to the clergy in various rites rather than making any creative contributions. Perhaps a thoughtful and concerned diaconate can move beyond such a merely traditional role.

Is there a place for the deacons to assist in discovering the forms and materials of worship which will best express the action of God on one hand and the proper response of the people on the other? The free churches, which have claimed to have no liturgy, have had one nevertheless, a liturgy built on habitual actions rather than serious thought and purpose. Consequently, our deepest convictions and our most enlightened understandings of the gospel are often obscured by patterns of worship which have grown up willy-nilly.

We need to ask how the rehearsal of the mighty deeds of God by word and act in worship can become effective in drawing the non-Christian to salvation and inspiring the Christian to praise and loving service.

Many have been probing for ways that will express both the Good News to our age and the devotion of the modern Christians. The free churches, whose worship is sometimes described as a group of people gathered to watch the minister conduct his private devotions in public, should take some time to think their way into the renewal of worship. If on the one hand we cannot accept the jazz mass and if on the other hand we believe our traditional forms are not meeting the people of today, where are we?

All kinds of gimmicks are being tried to update worship, but real progress shall have come when we seriously bring the gospel and the actual life of the people together. Then worship will be the vehicle for the adoration, reverence, contrition, petition, intercession, and obedience that accords with the needs, the abilities, and concerns of the people in our day.

Perhaps we should also ask whether the time we give to worship is the proper one for our day. Many can remember the days of World War II when some worship services were geared to the changing shifts at the local aircraft plant or shipyard. The crisis of war passed and we returned to normality, or did we? A few churches, looking at shortened workweeks, sabbatical leaves for factory workers, and the generally increased amount of self-directed time, have added church services on Thursday or Friday evening in the sanctuary, at the beach, or in the mountains. Some pastors have moved prayer meeting for the men to the early hours of the morning and for women to the coffee break. After all, the purpose is not to preserve the sanctity of a particular hour but the life of devotion, witness, and service of the people of God.

Perhaps the deacons should consider how the various groups of the community might be served in the worship service. Even the small church which meets twice on Sunday and once during the week can arrange to have each service different in form and in the worship materials used. This is simply to acknowledge that people are different. Some people will enter readily into the free, almost ecstatic expression of the newer groups while some will prefer a more ordered or even liturgical service. For many people worship consists of a study of the Scriptures, while for others its heart is in ritual or exhortation. Why should not the various services and meetings of the church provide with thoughtful care for persons rather than merely follow the preacher's inclination to one form of worship or another? We frequently confuse the question of "integrity of ministry" with matters of personal taste rather than the integrity of the gospel and the response of the people.

Immediately following World War II, one church involved its laity in a ministry to a variety of nationalities through classes in citizenship, language, and the Bible. Worship services were held in different languages. We should also give credit to the church that ministers in a variety of ways to the various groups that are less dramatically visible around the churches of today. Persons can be expected to mature more rapidly in the expression of their faith when the possibility for growth exists in a structured program that allows for several expressions of faith and obedience within the church.

The diaconate should be concerned that the Christian witness is not held aloof from persons. Some churches use the Sector Zone Plan gatherings in order to develop small study and discussion groups. (See the discussion of this plan in Chapter 5.) Under the pastor or a capable lay person, Christians and nearby non-Christians alike share in discussing the troublesome issues of life in the light of the gospel.

Similar groups can sometimes be formed on the basis of a common occupation or position in life, or from a cross section of the community. These, too, try to deal with real issues and then make studied attempts to focus the light of the gospel upon them. The pastor and the various denominational offices can be called upon for resource materials. Frequently groups such as these are formed on other than geographical bases because the persons one associates with most frequently or with whose lives his own is most intertwined are people who share the same work, recreation, or mutual responsibilities. These may be one's neighbors even more precisely than the couple next door.

Coffee houses under church sponsorship provide a time and place where young people may talk freely about their doubts and fears and where they may often be engaged in conversation concerning the faith. Neutral buildings or rooms have been opened outside the church edifice where people, Christians and non-Christians alike, may discuss under Christian auspices the deeper issues and tensions of life. Those who remain outside the church are often surprised to discover that Christians also share in the problems and ambiguities of life and that the church holds them in its concern.

Some pastors have found an exciting witness in classes for those who are not Christians but who have been encountered by the people of the church in visitation or in the ordinary round of life. Spontaneous discussion enables persons to raise their doubts and face their questions honestly before publicly committing themselves to Christ.

Then there is the church where the diaconate wondered how to expand its missionary interest in its small community on the plains. The deacons led in planting a "house church" in a home in a little crossroads community almost twenty miles away where there never can be an established church in the traditional pattern. There is not much preaching there because it is largely a lay venture, but there is fellowship, study, and witness in the name of Christ. A deacon in another church mentioned this "house church" idea to a woman concerned for the restless, aimless women of her community. She established one group, and two more soon resulted to help meet the needs for ministry.

When the diaconate is concerned with getting the gospel to where people are, Christians are strengthened in the process and decisions result, though not always in a spectacular manner, because the newer styles of ministry are often directed toward the unreached, the alienated, or the indifferent. Often the very right to witness must be won slowly and laboriously, but with concern and hope in the power of the Spirit of God. A new generation is asking new questions in new ways but with minimal preparation to aid in the search for answers. Hence, the diaconate should always be concerned that no group be overlooked, no area of life ignored.

In a surprising way five consultations of representative American Baptists in various parts of the nation said that the deacons should develop ways to renew the ties between the churches. If we think the concept of fellowship has been watered down to mere "togetherness" in the local church, the practice of fellowship between churches has simply disappeared. By losing the strong sense of interdependence and unity in Jesus Christ which the early churches on this continent experienced, we have made it easy to split from churches of like faith and practice and to believe our enemies rather than our fellows in the household of faith. For all too many persons the independent spirit presents the spectacle of people who worship a Lord of confusion in a spirit of arrogant division. It is scarcely pertinent to place the blame for our present fragmentation. It is time, rather, to bear an humble witness in daily life that God has made of diverse people one body in Christ.

Serious difficulties arise when a church overemphasizes its autonomy. For one thing, it is simply too easy to be complacent, self-assured, arrogant, and even in error when we stand aloof from those who might challenge us, correct us, and instruct us. In the second place, a church that stands alone is readily made to feel threatened and futile by the challenge of the recalcitrant age to which it is supposed to minister. It cannot experience the strength which is available in the help, encouragement, and support of mutual concern. Third, churches can pull away from each other, repudiate each other's ministry, and add to the fragmentation of the Body of Christ without compunction when they have not known each other. Fourth, and most important, under the guise of strengthening the work of Christ in this way or that, the precise ministry that Christ gave to the church is really weakened almost beyond repair by the piecemeal efforts of solitary congregations acting independently of each other.

The minutes of the early Baptist associations make interesting reading. The churches of the Philadelphia Association, for instance, believed in the autonomy of the local church in a sense that the validity of its ministries did not depend on a bishop or hierarchy but on the presence of the Spirit of God in the midst of his people. At the same time they believed and practiced the interdependence of the churches. It was not thought to be a strange thing for a local congregation to ask the association for counsel on its internal needs. The messengers to the sessions then prayerfully searched the Scriptures, their own understanding and experience, and sent their suggestions back to the church. The suggestions were not binding, but the interest and labors of the association made the congregation consider the counsel seriously.

What could result if the diaconate in the various churches of an association determined to make that organization come alive? In recent years the deacons of the Philadelphia Association have had a series of training conferences which have sharpened their interest and skills and have built bridges between some of the churches. The resulting counsel and shared concern has been helpful to many.

This kind of relationship might hasten the day when associations could take some initiative in the extension of the church. Few congregations are strong enough to bring a new church into existence, but several churches, working cooperatively, might survey an area, secure a working nucleus, perhaps release a number of families to be a core membership, and provide the initial funds. National, state, and city offices of the denomination have a wealth of experience to put at the disposal of interested churches.

Then it is rare for a church not to have members who are at the eye of the storm in the troublesome issues and tasks of modern life, but seldom does one church have a sufficient number of these to form a supportive group. The diaconate in several churches of an association might form *ad hoc* groups to probe the issues of the times for the good of the persons so involved in order to give some direction to the concerned community of faith.

At least one association program committee took its cue from the German Kirchentag, a movement known to many because of the enormous mass meetings which are held every few years. What is not so visible is the study that goes on across the nation for months before the Kirchentag ("church day") as small groups wrestle with the very practical, earthy problems which they face in the world they know. The great days of the Kirchentag then provide the people with opportunities for worship and further study within the wider fellowship. Differing views inevitably appear, so a high degree of maturity is necessary as all those present search for the mind of Christ. The association in question chose a theme for study, and suggested resources to be used in the local churches in preparation for the wider discussion at its annual meeting.

There is also a growing concern among thoughtful lay people that Christians of the wider fellowship learn to work together. Roman Catholics, Orthodox, and Protestants in many parts of Europe learned how much they had in common in their faith under the pressure of suffering during World War II. This has not been forgotten, and here and there throughout Europe there is cooperation at the local level in meeting the common needs of men. For example, in a French city a priest and a minister of the Reformed Church discovered that the Communists were without strength because they could not offer the people anything greater than the concerned care of the combined efforts of the Christians.

Whatever one's personal position may be concerning the ecumenical movement and the widely diverse views of its members, it has, in fact, brought the differences between the various communions out into the open for discussion. Each group has had its own witness to bring to all the others. Differences there are, and differences there will remain. John Wesley was aware of these, but his desire to surmount the differences was shown in the letter he wrote to Henry Venn:

> I am not satisfied with "Be very civil to Methodists, but have nothing to do with them." No. I desire to have a league offensive and defensive with every soldier of Christ. We have not only one faith, one hope, one Lord, but are directly engaged in one warfare.[1]

This kind of awareness will enable the diaconate to help the

[1] John Telford, ed., *The Letters of the Rev. John Wesley,* 8 vols. (London: Epworth Press, 1931), Vol. IV, p. 218.

congregation to understand how important is the contribution which they, other churches, and other communions, bring to the total Christian cause.

Perhaps the time has come to ask a new question about the diaconate. If we are correct in stating that all the ministries of the church are to be expressive of the ministry of Christ and that this is best demonstrated in a servant role, we may have deacons around us who have not been recognized. We have suggested some ministries which are not quite traditional for the deacon — now we suggest some nontraditional deacons who nevertheless are fulfilling the servant role.

One step toward an expanding view of the deacon is to think of those outside the established boards of the church who may, in truth, be serving Christ in very special ways. The care for the welfare of individuals, once largely in the hands of the home and the church, is now under the control of other groups and agencies. But Christians still work there, living out their Christian commitment as doctors, nurses, counselors, social workers, technicians, teachers, civic employees, and so on. When their work is performed as Christian commitment, theirs is a diaconal ministry. Perhaps they should be recognized as deacons, although of a different order and with responsibilities differing from those who work within the institutional structures of the church.

A second way this may come about is for the diaconate to recognize needs in the church and out of it which call for special ministries and to ask the church to set persons aside to meet them. For example, we have noted the church which was not convinced that community assistance in the area of mental and emotional health met all the needs of those who sought help. Qualified persons in the congregation were recruited to counsel in such things as health, finance, home management, job training, and many other areas. Again, we have not called such people deacons but their service is in a true succession of diaconal work.

To give this kind of person official or quasi-official position would do several things. First, it would give the congregation a sense of identification with some of its own members who are expressing the love of Christ in service. Second, there would accrue to the individual an awareness of the support of the people of God for him in his ministry. Third, individually and collectively, the persons so engaged could share from their vantage point with the diaconate and other boards the reality of the need and the possibilities for the Christian witness of the congregation. The diaconate then would be in a position to think more realistically about the training and supportive relationships which might be helpful to those engaged in other ministries.

One church underscores the fact that every Christian is a deacon, a servant, by asking each of its members to hold a position of responsibility in the community as a service to Christ. This brings into sharp focus the reality that the decisions and acts of the Christian in the flow of our common life may be significant bits of evidence before the world of the saving grace and the lordship of Jesus Christ.

For Further Consideration

1. What should the leaders of your church know about the congregation in order to give more effective guidance for its inner strengthening and public ministry?
2. How would you go about determining groups and issues in your community to which your church should address its ministry?
3. What is worship? How may worship in your church be made more expressive of the gospel and the life of the people?

MOVING INTO THE FUTURE

Obviously it is impossible for a board of deacons to do all that has been outlined in these pages; and at best, these have been the scantiest of hints. When we ask how the servant concept works out in detail, we are compelled to confess our shadowy understanding and our doubts. Nevertheless, we must get on with the work of our Lord now, and right on into the future.

The task of the diaconate is particularly challenging when things are in a state of flux. It does not take an unusually perceptive individual to say that everything is changing, but only a person of genuine insight can tell what the major thrusts of change really are and at what rate they are occurring. Astute men will see that different kinds of change come to varying places and peoples at different tempos and that responses may differ according to each situation.

If few of us can grasp the complexity of the changes which throng in upon us, fewer still can claim the creativity to unravel what it all means for the forms of life and ministry which should characterize the church in the years to come. A certain brooding, daring, consecrated creativity will be essential to grasp what the congregation of believers must do if the gospel of Christ is to be held in dynamic confrontation with our day. Change, like a wildfire running across the plains, cannot be ignored. It touches the lives of men and cultures, and every change, as well as every person caught up in our changing age, is a challenge to the people of God to hold the gospel in contact with every need of men. The deacons should see themselves as those who are commissioned to give leadership to the church in this, the most challenging of eras.

No one can release the diaconate from its leadership role. No books, no series of conferences, no denominational leaders, however pertinent their help, can give the answers to every local church. Increasingly the creative response to the actual needs of those about us must come from within each congregation. Only those who are deeply enmeshed in the life of a local church can determine what their congregation should do. It is their responsibility to know their world, their community, and their faith, and to bring them all together.

The members of a congregation must be led to consider seriously what it means to be the church in a world like the one which surrounds them. They should plan to witness in simplicity and yet with sophistication. Our generation is educated to a higher level than has ever been known, but intellectuals are viewed with suspicion by many. The extremes of affluence and poverty, learning and ignorance, alertness and dull apathy will continue to face us. Great good is certain to continue and so is evil – both in ever-changing patterns.

Here is something terrifying for the church when its emotional ties to the past seem threatened. At the same time there is something exhilarating and exciting about this era because new frontiers are ever flinging their challenges at us. If the church is static and moribund today, it is because we have lost our vision and a flexibility which the early Christians seem to have possessed.

The diaconate is, in a sense, the conservator of the past, holding in its role as a steward of the best practices and traditions of the church of the ages that which is lasting, eternal, and valid in the Christian faith. At the same time the deacons must discern carefully between the heart of the faith and the accretions of the years if they are to give leadership to change.

Many corporations have permanent offices to deal with the constant need for organizational adjustments which the changing technologies and shifting patterns of modern life impose on them. Perhaps the diaconate can become a built-in agent of change providing a continuity of purpose springing from deep and permanent relationships while at the same time it looks for the strategic moves which must be plotted for tomorrow's ministry. If, as some scientists maintain, we can now predict what our world will be like in fifty years, the church can no longer wait for the modes of its witness and the forms of its life to be thrust on it by forces outside the concern of the Christian faith. The church should plot the needs that may arise and call for the changes which ought to be made, plan for them, and carry them out to the best of its ability.

Many churches set aside a part of the annual planning conference to brainstorm about what the church should do in the future. The results, including the wildest suggestions, are recorded, sifted out, and then studied for whatever hint they may offer concerning future action. One board of deacons has the practice of appointing two men every few months to bring in several of their best suggestions for expanding the ministry of the church. Many of the suggestions are filed for further discussion, and some are never used; but at least the pastor testifies that this procedure has helped his congregation to fill a ministry that is nearer to what it should be than would otherwise be true.

Any leader wishes that he could see into the future. The deacon is in the same position. If we read the New Testament correctly, God can move in many ways to produce change. For example, God's guidance was recognized when he gave instructions which Christians ratified by their deeds, or when he took the initiative through the corporate action of the church, or when he used a new situation to challenge his people to move forward, or as he gave one person a new ministry which the church later recognized as essential (see Acts 11:27-30; 13:1-3; 6:1-15; and 1 Corinthians 16:15, 16). Sometimes God's Spirit moved in the orderly channels of church life and sometimes in unexpected ways and places, as in the founding of the church at Antioch.

The early Christians were as human as we are. Change and expansion did not come easily or without sacrifice and even disagreement, because the path ahead was not that clear to them. But they moved ahead (see the story of the Jerusalem Council in Acts 15). It may be that God has other, and yet equally effective, ways of leading us in our generation as we try to face the troublesome issues, private and public, which face every man.

It is only right for the diaconate to help the church face the prophetic question: "What is God saying to us and to our day?" A group of professional men in a small eastern city asked a pastor to share with them in studying the Scriptures and the works of some of the leading contemporary theologians. Like many lay groups in other places, they began to ask the question, "What does all this mean for us now?" A practical, highly sophisticated technological age still asks this question. The prophet in our churches and society will always be aware of the power of sin to distort dreams and pervert the best of plans, but he is needed to help us retain the vision of the city of God while still working in the cities and towns of this world.

The modern deacon must be a planner as well as a leader. Dreams must be made to walk the streets in concrete programs designed to fulfill God's will. Objectives must be set for the church in its capacities as a fellowshiping, worshiping, studying, witnessing, and serving community. Paths toward the goals must be plotted. Resources should be evaluated and every effort made to have the plans provide creative opportunities for Christians to fulfill their commitment in a diaconal ministry that moves them beyond themselves.

Systems engineering has developed procedures by which the most complex problems can be studied from every feasible angle. This approach has given us a deeper understanding of the ways in which personnel may be deployed according to skills and how a task can be accomplished by breaking it down into sub-projects. These all, completed in logical sequence, contribute to the attainment of the major objective. Thousands of people, for example, work in many parts of the country on seemingly unrelated projects. But the results of their labors are brought together, fitted into place, and a spacecraft lifts off the earth. Deacons can join the pastor in leading the church to formulate the goals of life and ministry. The various tasks to be carried out will be determined, and every board, every activity, every skill will be drawn into a concentrated, unified endeavor.

The deacons cannot avoid the administrative task. Plans are not just to be formulated. They are shaped so that a work can be done effectively and efficiently. Many boards of deacons score superior grades in setting goals and laying plans, but then fail to carry them out. Sometimes this is because of a failure to set proper and possible objectives, sometimes because of the faulty setting of contributing projects, and sometimes because the deacons just do not act.

It may even be that failure in human relations is just as much to blame when plans go awry. The diaconate, not recognizing the need for significant groups of the congregation to be involved in the whole process of setting objectives, evaluating resources, and plotting a course of action, may try to press the pastor into the role of an autocratic director of church activities. The image of *the leader* has long since become anachronistic and the wise pastor refuses the role. So does the wise diaconate.

People feel responsible for that in which they are involved deeply by study, information, and active participation at every level of research, goal setting, project planning, and performance. Even though the diaconate may be immersed in the prophetic insight and dedication that sees many possible ministries, they will not expect their fellow Christians to make unquestioning leaps into the unknown. They, too, must traverse much the same path of study and research and concerned dreaming and planning until they accept this as a ministry of their own choosing. It is far better to include the necessary persons, who have insights and skills, in the very beginning of the process.

To follow such a pattern means that the deacons, while leading, will also be working alongside the membership, sharing their responsibilities, anxieties, and joys. It is not only good theology but also good administrative procedure for the leadership to work with the people in fulfilling their ministry.

The modern deacon must have a courage that grows out of a deep commitment to Jesus Christ. New challenges to the gospel, new claims upon the church, and unfamiliar ways of ministering will always be something of a threat. The only way out, if the church is to move out from its defensive position, is to turn the needs of our strange, new days into opportunities for ministry under the guidance of the risen Christ. He gave us the pattern for our service as he ministered lavishly, without regard to himself, even though he knew that his paths were leading to a cross.

The early church served uncalculatingly with results that ranged from enthusiastic acceptance to persecution and death. We, too, have been commissioned, as they were, to serve and bear witness. The seed we sow may bring forth an hundredfold, or sixtyfold, or not at all — but the seed must be sown in any event.

It takes courage to minister, whether the efforts be in traditional patterns or in modes quite new, when we know we will sometimes be in error and mistakes will be made. We can only commit ourselves and our efforts to the understanding of a gracious and forgiving Lord. His strength and presence, his grace and forgiveness are promised for the task. His acceptance and help will be given when we falter. Thus we can dare to serve even now in his name.

For Further Consideration

1. What do you feel is the will of God for your church in your community in your day?

APPENDIX 1
THE DEACONESS

Phoebe is called "a deaconess" in Romans 16:1, in the only place where the term appears in the New Testament. The word which later describes her as a "helper of many" was used more frequently of a patroness. Here it obviously indicates one who gave hospitality or some other assistance.

In spite of this reference, and even though we know of the work of the widows mentioned in 1 Timothy 5:9-10, there is no clear-cut evidence that a separate group known as deaconesses existed at that time. That Phoebe and others were serving in the life of the church is beyond question. We simply do not know whether this was based on some special authority.

Some have thought that the widows referred to in 1 Timothy 5:3-10 may be synonymous with deaconesses or that the reference to "the women" in 1 Timothy 3:11 may speak of deaconesses or the wives of deacons. We can readily understand that if these women began to fulfill certain specific functions in the church, their role would be gradually institutionalized.

That the church of the early postapostolic centuries did identify widows with the concept of the deaconess is indicated by the number of times the age of sixty from 1 Timothy 5:9 is mentioned in the writings from that era. The *Apostolic Constitutions* (VI. 17) says that a deaconess should be a chaste virgin or a widow "but once married, faithful, and well esteemed." [1] The Fourth Council of Carthage (ch. 12) spoke of widows and consecrated virgins.

At the beginning of the third century the deaconesses are seen as a strong order within the church. In the middle of that century, Eusebius speaks of them as poor women who were dependent on the support of the church. The Council of Nicea speaks only of deaconesses and the Council of Orleans in 533 referred to "widows who are called deaconesses." [2]

Evidence is limited that the deaconess submitted to some rite of ordination or installation. We do learn, however, that these women were to discharge the same care for the well-being of the poorer women in the fellowship as was given the men by the deacons. Then there came a time when the deaconesses were given some responsibility in the instruction of the catechumens. The Fourth Council of Carthage speaks of their being qualified to assist the unlearned candidate in how to answer the interrogatories in the baptismal service and how to live after baptism.

It also appears that the early prevalence of baptism by immersion, and the anointing of the whole body with oil which

[1] "Constitutions of the Holy Apostles" in *The Ante-Nicene Fathers,* Alexander Roberts and James Donaldson, eds. (New York: Charles Scribner's Sons, 1905), Vol. VII, p. 457.

[2] Charles Joseph Hefele, ed., *A History of the Christian Councils* (Edinburgh: T. and T. Clark, 1894), Vol. I, pp. 432, 433; Vol. IV, p. 187.

preceded it, rendered it a matter of propriety that the diaconal function in baptism should be performed by women. This may well have been one of the original duties of the deaconess. Other responsibilities differed from place to place. They are described variously as keeping the doors of the church, assigning seats in the church to new converts who were women, and being present at all interviews between a woman and a priest, bishop, or deacon.

It appears that the office of the deaconess began to disappear as adult baptism became less common. The order of deaconesses died out in the Eastern Church by the eighth century even though the title continued to be given as an honor to certain nuns. In the Roman Church the office continued in spite of the hostility of some of the Councils (Synod of Epaon in 517 and Second Synod of Orleans in 533), but by the end of another nine hundred years the deaconesses had died out as a separate order and their places were taken by cloistered nuns.

In more modern times the deaconess has appeared among Protestants both as a member of a professional order and as a volunteer worker. There were deaconesses among the early Mennonites in Holland. Thomas Cartwright and Walter Travers in 1575 spoke of ". . . deacons of both sorts, namely men and women."[3] In 1823 and 1832, Pastor Theodor Fliedner, a Lutheran, saw deaconesses in action, and in 1836 he established the first institution for the special training of church women "for works of mercy in the name of Christ" at Kaiserwerth, Germany. He influenced the Church of Scotland in establishing an order in 1887-88. By 1950, of the 60,000

[3] Thomas Cartwright and Walter Travers, "A Full and Plain Declaration of Ecclesiastical Discipline out of the Word of God and of the Declining of the Church of England from the Same," cited by D. S. Schaff, "Deaconess" in *The New Schaff-Herzog Encyclopedia of Religious Knowledge,* Samuel Macauley Jackson, ed., (New York: Funk & Wagnalls, 1909), Vol. III, p. 374.

deaconesses in the world, most were Lutheran and represented many countries, including 1,500 deaconesses listed in the United States.[4] In the United States they are to be found in Methodist, Episcopal, Presbyterian, and Lutheran churches.

During the height of interest in the formation of the sisterhoods, a Baptist Deaconesses' Society was formed in New York in 1895. The first graduates, called sisters and wearing a distinctive garb, began work in 1897. Several other similar efforts were made in Chicago, Philadelphia, and Dayton in the latter years of the nineteenth century.

The strongest such efforts among the Baptists have been carried out by the German Baptist deaconesses, whose work, principally in relieving need, nursing, social work, and Christian education, has been extremely beneficial. But this kind of movement has never had the depth of acceptance in the United States that it still bears in Europe.

In most Baptist churches of the United States, the deaconess is a volunteer who is chosen by the church in the same manner as other officers. Her primary responsibility is to serve church people within the church fellowship. Where this position is accepted, the deaconess has fallen quite naturally into somewhat the same pattern as existed in some sections of the early church.

An increasing number of churches have the deacons and deaconesses meet in joint sessions with some regularity. This proves enriching to the life of the church. A small, but growing trend is to assign to the deaconesses the same functions as the deacons in all of their duties.

It may be that the important question is not whether women should hold positions in the church but whether the modern church can fulfill its ministry without them.

[4] E. Theodore Bachmann, "Deaconesses" in *Twentieth Century Encyclopedia of Religious Knowledge,* Lefferts A. Loetscher, ed. (Grand Rapids, Mich.: Baker Book House, 1955), Vol. I, p. 322.

APPENDIX 2
ONE BOARD FOR A CHURCH

There are many churches where a single board oversees the total program of the congregation. Often this group is referred to as the deacons, the diaconate, the official board, the board of directors, or some such title. Many of the newer churches adopt this pattern for rather obvious reasons, but it is not unknown for churches of longer history and larger congregations to move toward the one-board plan.

The concern of this book has been with those who perform and lead in the diaconal work of the church regardless of the title given them. Where fitting, the title of "deacon" should be used and interpreted. It must be said that the use of the title retains contact both with good biblical, historical roots and with the practice of sister congregations today.

Among the reasons given for adopting the one-board system

are: (a) it utilizes the best of leadership from among a small group of people; (b) it is more efficient to have the total program under a single board rather than to divide responsibilities among several discrete groups which often become competitive; (c) it is good to have all people in policy-making positions on one board to provide agreement on implementation and financing as well as on policy; (d) the plan makes possible the same standards for board membership for everyone who shapes the life of the congregation; (e) the membership of one board can provide a cross section of the congregation more readily than is possible with several boards; and (f) the minister is not the only link between the several programs and various phases of the life of the church.

Among the reasons which may be advanced against this plan are: (a) it is possible for power to become too centralized; (b) fewer people will be actively involved, and hence actively supporting the work in only one board; (c) a few strong persons on one central board can easily dominate the total program so that the work of the church may be thrown out of balance; (d) something is lost by way of checks and balances; and (e) the work of the board can include so many details that it will never get on to the major concerns it should face.

Discussion can go on at great length about the strengths and weaknesses of varying organizational patterns. Obviously, the particular polity adopted by a church will be no stronger than the ability and the commitment of the people involved. In either plan it is essential that there be united dreaming, planning, and serving in the work of Christ. This unity seems to be implied in the one-board system. Churches with other structures of organization have supplied this unity by means of an advisory board, or an executive committee composed of the moderator, clerk, treasurer, pastor, and the chairman of the major boards, so that the pastor is not the only tie that holds the entire program together.

The average church will want to provide for leadership in finances and property, missions, evangelism and fellowship, Christian education, and worship. Each emphasis may be represented on a single board by one, two, three, or more persons, depending on the size of the congregation and the nature of the program which is projected. In some churches a deacon will have a committee chosen from the membership working with him in one or another of the areas of interest. For example, several phases of Christian education could be represented by members of various departments working with a deacon as chairman. He in turn represents the total Christian education program on the diaconate. Thus there is built a tie between the wide range of programs and ministries which fill the life of the modern church.

This plan makes it imperative that a nominating committee be aware of the responsibilities of the various committees because people must be nominated according to the needs of the church and in keeping with their capabilities.

The one board may well be called the board of deacons, even though the traditional diaconal ministry is delegated to a subcommittee chaired by a deacon. Earlier studies have prepared us to accept this wider concept as proper for the diaconate since the service of the early Christian community seems to have ranged over the entire spectrum of human need.

In the one-board plan the various subcommittees will find their guidance from the proper national and state agencies of their denomination. They should become familiar with the materials that are applicable to their responsibilities.

There is no lack of guidance available to individual boards and committees. It falls to the pastor and the leaders of the local church to select those programs and materials which meet their needs, adapt them where necessary, and calendar them in a realistic way. Their task is to create a coherent, comprehensive, and relevant program that will truly represent the meaning of the gospel to the membership and to the world. To do this will make of many interests one ministry.

SELECTED BIBLIOGRAPHY

The Church and its Mission

A few of the many books resulting from a renewed interest in the nature and work of the church. Some, such as those by Handy and Rutenber, have been widely used in study groups. Much of the material in the others can be adapted. All will repay study.

Brister, C. W., *Pastoral Care in the Church.* New York: Harper & Row, Publishers, Inc., 1964. 262 pp.

Brunner, Heinrich Emil, *The Misunderstanding of the Church.* Philadelphia: The Westminster Press, 1953. 132 pp.

Flew, Robert Newton, *Jesus and His Church: A Study of the Idea of the Ecclesia in the New Testament.* Nashville: Abingdon Press, 1938. 275 pp.

Handy, Robert, *Members One of Another: studies in the nature of the church as it relates to evangelism.* Valley Forge: The Judson Press, 1959. 114 pp.

McCord, James I. and Parker, T. H. L., eds., *Service in Christ.* London: Epworth Press, 1966. 233 pp.
Minear, Paul Sevier, *Images of the Church in the New Testament.* Philadelphia: The Westminster Press, 1960. 294 pp.
Payne, Ernest, *The Fellowship of Believers.* London: Carey Kingsgate Press, 1952. 168 pp.
Rutenber, Culbert G. *The Reconciling Gospel.* Valley Forge: The Judson Press, 1960. 183 pp.
Welch, Claude, *The Reality of the Church.* New York: Charles Scribner's Sons, 1958. 254 pp.
Walton, Robert C., *The Gathered Community.* London: Carey Kingsgate Press, 1946. 184 pp.

The Church and Its Community

Only three out of a wealth of books which can help a church determine the possible ministries it might undertake. The first tells of creative ministries in rural churches. The latter two, while dated, give some feeling for the kind of information a congregation may want to have as a foundation for its planning.

Bockelman, Wilfred, *On Good Soil.* New York: Friendship Press, 1959. 173 pp.
Leiffer, Murray H., *The Effective City Church.* Nashville: Abingdon Press, 1949. 232 pp.
Sanderson, Ross, *The Church Serves the Changing City.* New York: Harper & Row, Publishers, Inc., 1955. 252 pp.

The Church and Communication

A deepened interest in the ministry of the church has stimulated a concern about how the gospel may be communicated in our age. Here are some of many works which have appeared.

DeWire, Harry A., *The Christian as Communicator.* Philadelphia: The Westminster Press, 1960. 198 pp.
Kraemer, Hendrik, *The Communication of the Christian Faith.* Philadelphia: The Westminster Press, 1956. 128 pp.
Sellers, James, *The Outsider and the Word of God: a Study in Christian Communication.* Nashville: Abingdon Press, 1961. 240 pp.

The Ordinances

Three books on the ordinances: the first by the principal of Spurgeon's College in London, the second by a group of British Baptist ministers who share the results of their disciplined study, and the third is a rewarding study of the words of our Lord as they relate to the communion.

Beasley-Murray, George Raymond, *Baptism in the New Testament.* London: Macmillan & Company, Ltd., and New York: St. Martin's Press, Inc., 1962. 424 pp.

Gilmore, Alec, ed., *Christian Baptism.* Valley Forge: The Judson Press, 1959. 343 pp.

Jeremias, Joachim, *The Eucharistic Words of Jesus.* New York: The Macmillan Company, 1955. 196 pp.

Baptist History and Polity

A group of books by Baptists who share their thought and study with those who want to know more about the Baptist heritage. They are worthy of study.

Asquith, Glenn, H., *Church Officers at Work.* Valley Forge: The Judson Press, 1951. 92 pp.

Lumpkin, William L., *Baptist Confessions of Faith.* Valley Forge: The Judson Press, 1959. 430 pp.

Maring, Norman H., and Hudson, Winthrop S., *A Baptist Manual of Polity and Practice.* Valley Forge: The Judson Press, 1963. 237 pp.

Torbet, Robert G., *A History of the Baptists,* rev. ed. Valley Forge: The Judson Press, 1963, 538 pp.

New Forms of Ministry

An increasing number of books reflect the efforts being made to relate the church to the realities of our day. These are a sampling to indicate some of the ways churches are expressing their freedom to express their deepest concerns for ministry.

Clark, M. E., Malcomson, W. L., and Molton, W. L., eds., *The Church Creative.* Nashville: Abingdon Press, 1967. 208 pp.

Clemmons, Robert S., *Education for Churchmanship.* Nashville: Abingdon Press, 1966. 205 pp.

Fisher, Wallace E., *From Tradition to Mission.* Nashville: Abingdon Press, 1965. 208 pp.

O'Connor, Elizabeth, *Call to Commitment.* New York: Harper & Row, Publishers, Inc., 1963. 205 pp.

Raines, Robert A., *New Life in the Church.* New York: Harper & Row, Publishers, Inc., 1961. 155 pp.

INDEX